Etiquette Lessons

Etiquette Lessons

Girls & Boys at the Table
Children and Youth Ages 5–12

Teens at the Table
Young Adults Ages 13–19

Part I: Table Manners & Social Behavior
Part II: American Cotillion

Teresa Kathryn Grisinger Reilly

iUniverse, Inc.
New York Lincoln Shanghai

Etiquette Lessons
Girls & Boys at the Table
Children and Youth Ages 5–12
Teens at the Table
Young Adults Ages 13–19

iUniverse books may be ordered through booksellers or by contacting:

iUniverse
2021 Pine Lake Road, Suite 100
Lincoln, NE 68512
www.iuniverse.com
1-800-Authors (1-800-288-4677)

Girls & Boys at the Table, Teens at the Table and American Cotillion also available for the civilized child at: www.etiquettelessons.com

ISBN-13: 978-0-595-33198-7 (pbk)
ISBN-13: 978-0-595-77983-3 (ebk)
ISBN-10: 0-595-33198-X (pbk)
ISBN-10: 0-595-77983-2 (ebk)

Printed in the United States of America

In Peace through Charm and Social Grace,
We Celebrate the Human Race. TKGR

Acknowledgements

I wish to thank my parents, Mr. and Mrs. Donald Charles Grisinger and Dorothy Mae Hendriks Grisinger for their love and for setting high standards. I thank my dear husband, Mr. Harold Lincoln Reilly, for unselfishly providing financial and technical aid needed to write, publish, and market this work. I thank our children, Rose Leilani and Gloria Tiare, for their grace and for illuminating a creative path for the child in me to myself as their mother, into the community as a volunteer and now to children everywhere as an educator and entrepreneur.

I am very thankful to Mrs. Jacqui Bruschweiler—a steadfast, knowledgeable friend and hostess, for helpful suggestions, cuisine expertise, good cooking, and cheerful assistance with hundreds of pilot lessons.

I am also very grateful to the educators who found merit and timeliness in my ideas and first introduced my programs into classrooms: Dr. Melissa Nurrenbrock, Head of School, Genesis Preparatory, Mrs. Debbie Lees, Genesis Dean of Students, Mrs. Catherine Zandecki, Principal, Genesis Elementary School, Principals Gail Gilmore, R.N., and Rene Hensley, R.N. and Middle School Director, Kelly Zenchuk of World of Knowledge, Montessori School and Mrs. Gillian Davis, A.R.A.D., Centre for Dance, Drama, Music and Martial Arts, Port Richey, Florida, USA.

Kudos to Dave & Terry League of www.leaguecomputers.com for creative, technical and marketing support giving www.etiquettelessons.com a viable global presence.

Contents

Part II
American Cotillion

Foreword

American families are good neighbors and hardworking, responsible citizens. Parents strive to give their children a good start in life, passing basic table manners and good behavior from one generation to the next. Due to the pace of modern life, there is little time for practical application of the finer points of etiquette. Details tend to become superfluous and gradually forgotten. Busy parents can't stop this trend; grandparents, aunts and uncles may not be there to help either. Busy families have few opportunities for organized etiquette instruction and practice at home. Now children can learn etiquette and practice regularly with their classmates at school.

Etiquette Lessons held in the classroom or after school with instructors and classmates will reinforce basics learned at home. What's more, no matter what their previous, personal exposure may be, students who receive *Etiquette Lessons:* Girls & Boys at the Table and Teens at the Table as standardized instruction in good table manners and social behavior will advance together from the common experience. Etiquette instruction in the classroom will get lasting results. It will reestablish the finer points of etiquette and good behavior in American culture as parts of a complete education. In addition, students will learn dining tips and sample some delicacies and gourmet foods served as the healthy snack with each lesson.

Fashion, style and taste may modify etiquette instruction, but the general message will always be the same: This is how it's done. That message should be received far in advance of a formal invitation to dine. When the message is received in class, students conform as a group. They begin helping each other or competing for success spontaneously, as with any other class work. Students are eager to answer the instructor's questions. To their delight, they recognize most of what they already know and they enjoy adding to it. Unlike sessions at home, which may be frustrating for adults and embarrassing to youngsters, Etiquette Lessons in school are validating, confirming and fun for everyone.

To the best of my knowledge, this is the first comprehensive etiquette program designed for use in school classrooms with children grades K-12. Etiquette Lessons contains lesson scripts including: "Girls & Boys at the Table," "Teens at the Table, Part I, "Table Manners and Good Social Behavior," and Part II, "American Cotillion." Lessons are read to students as they work through activities. Instructors quiz students frequently. Questions and answers are provided after each lesson. Inexpensive and easily acquired supplies needed are listed in the Lesson Guide. Lessons are prepared in 15-minute segments which can be worked into the school day along with a light snack, after school, as summer programs or even at home.

Teresa Kathryn Grisinger Reilly, Director
etiquettelessons.com

Introduction

A word to the Girls & Boys

The word *etiquette* means *"conventional requirements as to proper social behavior."* Learning etiquette will help you to *fit in* socially. It will modify your behavior so that you probably won't offend anyone and you will never have to feel embarrassed because you don't know what to do. Just as in sports, ballet, or any other discipline—like driving a car for example—knowing the rules gives us freedom to really enjoy the game, the dance, or the road. With practice, we perfect our skills. We work with coaches, directors, and teammates to apply the rules. We learn how to channel our strengths toward team goals. Likewise, as you master the rules of etiquette, gaining confidence in your skills, you will soon conform to the roles of ladies and gentlemen. Once there, with rude language and behavior left behind, your best traits will shine through.

During this course of lessons in etiquette, the class will be a virtual dining room. In addition to learning how to eat properly, or *dine*, you will learn how to interact with others in social situations. For example, you will learn roles played by ladies and gentlemen being seated at the dining table. You will also learn to listen to others, become aware of their concerns, be considerate, quick to respond and even anticipate their needs. These are some of the manners often referred to as "social graces." Practice your social graces at every opportunity with classmates and family. Soon you will be at ease dining and socializing with others.

Etiquette Lessons

Girls & Boys at the Table

Girls & Boys at the Table

Lesson Guide

Welcome to *Girls and Boys at the Table Etiquette Lessons*! These lessons were designed for classes of 12 to 24 students, with a time allotment of 45 minutes each. Lessons contain a lecture and a demonstration, writing and drawing activities, food service, eating, and clearing tables. Lessons are written in scripts for the instructor to read while students work through activities in three 15-minute segments per lesson—one lesson per class. It is appropriate for students in grades K through 5th grade. (Instructors will need assistance serving more than 12 students.) Before class begins, place tableware on a side table and put a placemat on the table for each student. Each lesson includes a healthy snack prepared beforehand and served in the later part of the class, after the table is set or written activities are completed. Each lesson ends with a quiz. Food should be kept fresh or warm and out of sight until served. Always serve from the left and clear from the right. For best results, instructor and assistants should look formal by wearing a white blouse or shirt with a black skirt or slacks or a basic black or dark dress with pearl accessories.

Furniture Required

Students may use their own desktop at school or sit at a cafeteria table, picnic bench or dining table. The instructor will also need a table for the display of dishes, flatware, cups and napkins and a staging area for food with a refrigerator nearby. A white board with low-odor markers and two telephone headsets will come in handy.

Supplies Needed

The instructor will read Lesson Scripts from this book. Instructor will also need: one serving tray, tongs, a ladle, a pitcher, and a breadbasket for each 12 students. The students will need plain white napkins, paper place mats, paper plates, 6" desert plates (to be used as bread plates), 6" doilies for appetizer service, plastic cups, bowls for soup, plastic knives, forks and spoons, 3X5" index cards, crayons or pens, and a ball to toss around.

Food Service for Lesson One

Serve melon such as cantaloupe, honeydew or watermelon, sliced in long crescent or triangle shapes approximately 1/4 inch thick. Students may have second servings. Serve one at a time with tongs. The melon is used to practice use of the fork and knife for slicing and eating bite-sized pieces of steak or turkey. This will be repeated often during the course, using different types of melon. Also serve graham crackers on the bread plate and lemonade or apple juice. Note: Lesson One focus is primarily on the *place setting*. However, the instructor will use this opportunity to observe students' eating habits and use of utensils.

Food Service for Lesson Two

This lesson calls for small dinner rolls, fresh and warm from the oven if possible, placed in a basket and served with tongs. Provide enough so each student may have several rolls. Place them one at a time on the bread plate. Also serve butter in balls or pats on a dish, and lemonade or apple juice.

Food Service for Lesson Three

As part of the discussion of difficult foods to eat, serve buttered spaghetti noodles with grated parmesan cheese, short breadsticks, and lemonade, apple juice or white grape juice. An exercise to demonstrate the art of conversation is performed with tossing the ball.

Food Service for Lesson Four

This is basically a writing lesson and does not require a place setting. You will need placemats, index cards, and pens or crayons. During the last 15 minutes, serve a small plate of "Funny Face Finger Food" appetizers. Make faces with items such as cream cheese and celery, baby carrots, Spanish olives, salami, crackers, raisins and pickles. Be creative! Use 6" desert plates with doilies.

Presentation of Etiquette Achievement Certificates

See "copy and print" sample Certificate
and
Order Instructions in back of book for additional
Certificates and Student Booklets.

Girls & Boys at the Table

Lesson 1: Meeting people, Place Settings, How to Use the Knife and Fork

Welcome to the class; now that we are here please be quiet and listen. We have a lot of material to cover in very little time. Let's start by getting to know each other's names. I am _____. You will notice that I have a title before my name. That is because I am an adult. We always put "Mrs.," "Mr.," or "Ms." in front of an adult's name. This is a way of showing respect. If you don't know the adult's name it is appropriate to call them Sir or Ma'am (for madam).

In fact, everyone has a title. Titles acknowledge an adult person's age and accomplishments. Titles help define who we are, while at the same time protecting our privacy. Sometimes children use their titles, too. If this were a formal occasion, like a wedding reception, you might be introduced with "Miss" or "Mister" before your first and last names. First names and nicknames are usually shared only with close family and friends at school.

Take turns telling us just your first names. Pay close attention because we are going to play a memory game next. We'll start with you. What is *your* name? If you already know each other, we'll use middle names.

Here's how we play the game...I will choose someone, then they have to tell me their name and the name of the person to their right and the person to their left, then call the name of someone else who will do the same until everyone has had a turn. OK? Any questions? I will start with *you*...

We always try to learn the names of the other people with whom we are dining. There are two reasons for this. Can anyone guess what they are? Yes, to make new friends, and also so that if we need something on the table that is not in front of us we can ask for it, using the name of the person closest to it. For example, "Kevin, please pass the butter." We ask others to pass things to us because it is considered rude to lean over the table or reach across in front of someone.

What are the magic words to use when asking for and receiving something? "Please" and "Thank you," of course. If someone says, "Thank you," to you for passing something to them, what should you say? That's right, "You're welcome." You know most of this already.

Our lesson for today is about Place Settings. "Place settings" define our personal space when we sit down to eat at the table. You will each learn to set your place at the table. Place settings can have a few pieces and be very simple for casual dining, or they can have a lot of pieces and be very fancy for formal dining. How many of you help set the table at home?

Traditionally, families sat at a table together for meals. At the table, families told each other stories about busy days, made announcements, asked questions, planned activities, or discussed news. Girls and boys learned family values at the table. Parents trained their children to be polite while they shared a meal and held a conversation. Most modern families don't have time for meals that include traditional etiquette training.

Today, we all have busy schedules and many of our meals are eaten "on the run." Meals are sometimes picked up at the drive-through window and eaten with our hands in the car, picnic style. Take-out finger food is very popular these days and television is watched during many meals and is the subject of conversation. How many eat pizza at least twice a month? It's true; most of us eat at least one meal with our hands each day.

I know that talking about food makes us hungry. Don't worry, we will have a little snack soon.

So why do we have to learn good table manners and etiquette? Because we also sometimes attend formal dining occasions, like Thanksgiving dinner or wedding receptions in fine restaurants and dining rooms, where we must know how to feed ourselves with flatware and behave properly. Also, because it is part of America's cultural heritage. Dining etiquette and good social behavior create a common language and forum for diverse ethnic groups to share. For example, here is a bit of everyday etiquette. If friends visit your home, invite them in, introduce them to your family, offer them a seat and a beverage. Most people appreciate a glass of ice water. This is the traditional routine for making people feel welcome, whether we are in a formal dining room or not.

Who can tell me what flatware is? "Flatware," "silverware," or "cutlery" refers to the knife, fork, and spoon you use to eat.

The basic formal place setting has 6 parts. Here is a rhyme to help you remember them :

The Place Setting Rhyme

Hey Diddle Diddle,
My plate in the Middle,
And we'll be eating soon.

My fork on the Left,
Below the bread plate,
Across from my cup and spoon.

My knife on the Right,
Its blade facing in,
And now we can begin.

TKGR

We have the plates and cups and everything else we need to make a place setting. First we will draw a picture of the rhyme so we know where everything goes in our Place Setting. Here is something for you to draw with on the paper placemat in front of you.

What comes first? Yes, the plate, so draw a circle the size of your plate. Then where does the fork go? Think of the rhyme again. Yes, on the left, below what? The bread plate, always on your left with the fork! So draw a fork and a smaller circle representing the bread plate above it on the left side of the plate.

What is across from the bread plate and fork? Ah, the cup and spoon, which go on the right! Draw a small circle for the cup and below it draw a spoon. What else is on the right? Yes, the knife! The knife lies between the plate and the spoon at the right of the plate. Who can tell me which way the blade should face, and why? Yes, it's facing the food, ready for use. Say the rhyme again. Commit it to memory. Say it at home.

Now we will put all the place setting pieces on our pictures. When it is your turn, please quietly go to the plates table and find what you need, come back and put them one piece at a time on your picture.

Once our places are set, we can have a little refreshment. For that we need something to protect our clothes from spills and crumbs falling into our lap. What do we need? Yes, that's right! The napkin, or "serviette," as they are sometimes called. It is normally found under the fork to the left of the plate. However one finds them folded in the shape of a bird sitting on the dinner plate, or even rolled-up and popping out of an empty goblet on the upper right side of the place setting.

When you sit down at the table, the first thing you do is open your napkin halfway and put it in your lap. If you must leave the table during a meal, place your napkin on your chair, not on the table. When you are done eating, pick up your napkin loosely and place it on the table to the left of your plate.

As the rhyme says, "Now we can begin." We are serving melon with today's lesson. Use the melon to practice your cutting and eating skills. All meats, such as steak, turkey, and fish, should be cut and eaten one bite at a time. Your knife and fork are used as extensions of your pointer fingers. Hold your fork without making a fist.

There are two different styles of cutting and eating. The style you use is a matter of personal choice. Both are perfectly acceptable. With both, use your fork to hold the meat in place while slicing-off a small piece. Use your knife in a stroking motion; not back and forth. (Author, Teresa Grisinger Reilly, is in agreement with Victorian, etiquette authority, Emily Post, in recommending you keep your fork in your left hand and simply pop that bite of meat into your mouth after cutting.) Known as "Continental Style," this method of cutting and eating, used in Europe and Canada is gaining popularity in America because it is quiet and requires less juggling of utensils than the "American Style" of cutting, in which one puts the knife down, placing the fork into the right hand after cutting each bite. Then one eats, places the fork back in the left hand, picks up the knife with the right, cuts another bite and repeats the process.

In the Continental Style...still holding the knife with your right hand and fork in your left hand, rest your wrists on the table edge while chewing or talking, and then proceed with cutting another piece of meat. With the tip of your knife, a bit of vegetables and potato could be placed on top of your bite of meat before it goes into your mouth. You should see the back of your hands, with pointer fingers extended, when looking down on this process. If you wish to drink from your beverage, place your knife (blade inward) along the top edge of your plate, lift your glass with your right hand, drink, and then return to the eating process. Of course, we hold our fork in our right hand to dine when we are not cutting.

When you are taking a break while dining, place your knife and fork in the shape of an X on your plate, fork prongs downward. This means "At rest."

Bite-sized pieces will allow you to participate in conversation without speaking with your mouth full. Stifle the urge to point with your knife or gesture with your fork as you speak.

When someone serves you, you should always try a few bites of each dish. You may discover some new favorite foods. Now we will each take a piece of melon and use our knife and fork to eat it. We will start each of our lessons with place settings and end with a snack.

When finished, place both the knife and fork diagonally across your plate like the red international symbol for "NO". This position tells your waitperson to remove your plate. It also helps to keep the flatware from falling off when your plate is removed. When leaving your place at the table, try to replace your chair so that it won't be in the way. That ends our first lesson.

(Lesson 1—Quiz Time)

Thank you for being quiet and cooperative during our etiquette lesson. Please do your share to help with clean up. I look forward to seeing you again at our next lesson.

Girls and Boys at the Table: Lesson One

Quiz

Questions and Answers

Question 1. What is the proper way to address an adult?
Answer: To show respect, children should address adults as "Ma'am," "Sir" or use their Surname with a title Like: Ms., Mr., Dr. or Captain Jones, etc.

Question 2. Where do I place my napkin if I must leave the table during a meal?
Answer: If I must leave the table during a meal, I place my napkin on the chair.

Question 3. What is the "at rest" position for my utensils when I am not eating?
Answer: In the shape of an "X" across my plate, as if to say, "X marks the spot, this is my treasure, do not remove it."

Question 4. How do I show that I am finished with my meal?
Answer: I place the knife and fork diagonally across my plate from upper left to lower right. On a clock's face this would be ten minutes before four o'clock, or twenty minutes after ten.

Question 5. Recite or write the "Place Setting Rhyme."
Answer:

Place Setting Rhyme

Hey Diddle Diddle,
My plate in the Middle,
And we'll be eating soon.

My fork on the Left,
Below the bread plate,
Across from my cup and spoon.

My knife on the Right,
Its blade facing in,
And now we can begin.

TKGR

Girls & Boys at the Table

Lesson 2: Name Cards, Gentlemen Assist Ladies with Chairs, Posture, Bread and Butter

Welcome back. Find your place at the table and we will begin. Today we are going to discuss things you can expect to happen before the meal is served in a formal dining room.

At formal dining occasions you will find a card with your name on it where the hostess or other people who planned the party want you to sit. It would be considered very rude to rearrange these cards. Seating alternates with boy, girl, boy, girl, etc. Why do you suppose that is? This seating arrangement provides more opportunities to make friends.

I should mention at this point that it is customary for gentlemen to help the ladies be seated. He would first help the lady seated to his right. This maneuver requires skill, tact, communication and teamwork.

Let's try it. Everyone stand up. Ladies, stand beside your chairs. If the chair is pushed in, gentlemen, pull the chair out and allow the lady to step in front of it. The gentleman takes the lady's chair by its back, saying, "May I help you?" He does this by gently pushing her chair under her as she sits down. When the chair touches the back of her knees, she starts to sit, putting one or both hands at her side, then firmly holds the seat of the chair as it is scooted under her. When the gentleman lets go of the chair, she can then finish pulling the chair under her while adjusting her distance from the table. What should she say then? Yes, "Thank you." Then the gentleman can seat himself.

Once you are seated, remember to sit with your back straight. Get plenty of sleep so that you do not need to prop yourselves up on elbows. Here is a rhyme to help you remember good posture

"__NAME__, __NAME__, strong and able. Keep your elbows off the table."

As you know, good posture is important. Who can tell me why? We look better sitting up straight, we probably won't drop food on our chest, and our meal will digest better if our stomach is not crushed under our ribs. Keeping your back straight, you can fold your hands in your lap or rest one wrist on the table while you are eating or at rest.

As soon as everyone is seated, at a formal dinner, waiters will appear and serve you. They may even put your napkin across your lap for you. They might pour water in your goblet (the biggest glass on the right in your place setting). They will offer you a dinner roll or some other form of bread, which would be placed on your bread plate, along with a pad or ball of butter.

It is appropriate to quietly say "Thank You" when a waiter gives you something. When you ask for something while dining, always say, "May I..." For example, "May I please have lemon in my water?" Now we will set our places and practice breaking, buttering and eating bite-sized pieces of bread.

First we will recite the place setting rhyme learned in lesson one. Who wants to recite the rhyme for us first?

Place Setting Rhyme

Hey Diddle Diddle,
My plate in the Middle,
And we'll be eating soon.

My fork on the Left,
Below the bread plate,
Across from my cup and spoon.

My knife on the Right,
Its blade facing in,
And now we can begin.

TKGR

Bread and rolls are eaten in bite-sized pieces, taken one at a time. Hold the bread in one hand and break off a piece. Apply a small amount of butter with your spreader, then put it in your mouth.

Often there will be a small knife lying across the bread plate for use in spreading butter. Appetizers are always served before the meal and may arrive in their own small plate and sit on top of your service plate or "charger" (the big plate in the middle). Sometimes they are on small platters which people pass around the table. Appetizers may be followed by a salad or a bowl of soup. Your waiter will provide you with any additional utensils needed and he will remove those that have been used or will not be needed.

When you are having salad, he will ask if you would like pepper ground fresh onto your salad with a huge hand-held pepper grinder. Salad is eaten with your salad fork, which is the smaller fork found to the left of your dinner fork. You may cut the larger pieces of salad with your fork and knife and then rest your knife on the edge of your serving plate underneath. Then put your fork in your right hand and use it to eat your salad. Salad dressing may be applied in the kitchen or delivered in a small cup "on the side," or next to your salad, so you can serve yourself.

Soup is eaten with a soupspoon, which is rounder and larger than a teaspoon. If your soup is served in a large, shallow soup plate, leave your spoon in it when you are resting or finished. If it is served in a smaller bowl or cup, place your spoon on the serving plate underneath.

To eat soup, tip the spoon away from you and fill it by moving it toward the back of the soup plate or bowl. Stir hot soup to cool it. Use the side of your soupspoon to cut vegetables, meat, cheese, etc., in your soup. Oyster crackers may be placed in the soup, one or two at a time. Keep the rest on your bread and butter plate. When just a small amount of soup is left, tip the bowl away from you and use the spoon to get the rest.

If the table is set without a bread plate and knife, put the bread and butter on the upper left side of your dinner plate. Use your dinner knife to spread the butter.

(Lesson 2—Quiz Time)

Thank you for being quiet and cooperative during our etiquette lesson. Please do your share to help with clean up. I look forward to seeing you again. That will end our lesson for today.

Girls and Boys at the Table: Lesson Two

Quiz

Questions and Answers

Question 1. T/F) It is acceptable to move your name card to another seat.

Answer: False. You must sit where your host has placed you.

Question 2. T/F) If there is no bread plate, we place bread and butter on the upper left quadrant of our dinner plate.

Answer: True, in this case, use your dinner knife for a spreader.

Question 3. T/F) Good posture has no effect on digestion.

Answer: False. Slumping allows no room for the stomach to work.

Question 4. T/F) Your bread plate is always on your left.

Answer: True. Your bread plate is on the left above your fork.

Question 5. Briefly describe how a gentleman assists a lady with her chair.

Answer: He says, "May I help you?" then he pulls the chair out from the table. She says, "Yes, please," steps in front of the chair, bends her knees and begins to sit down. He pushes the chair forward to touch the back of her legs while she takes the sides of the chair in her hands and pulls it under her as she sits. He then lets go of the chair and she says, "Thank you."

Girls & Boys at the Table

Lesson 3: Dining Tips, How to eat Spaghetti, Acceptable Language, Dining Conversation, Personality

Hello again. Please find the seat where your place card is waiting and stand behind your chair. Today we will start by setting the table. First we will say the Place Setting Rhyme. All together now…

Place Setting Rhyme

Hey Diddle Diddle..,
My plate in the Middle,
And we'll be eating soon.

My fork on the Left,
Below the bread plate,
Across from my cup and spoon.

My knife on the Right,
Its blade facing in,
And now we can begin.

TKGR

We'll start with the quietest, most attentive group. Please step, three at a time, to the plate table and get what you need. This will be a test for you. I'm sure you can do it. This time we won't draw the place setting. After you set your place, you may be seated.

In this lesson we will learn about foods that are difficult to eat. Can someone name a food you might call difficult to eat? Yes, That would include foods such as lobster and crab claws which require special utensils or fried chicken, and fish and chips, which are considered finger-foods unless they are served with a main course that requires the use of a knife and fork. Artichoke petals are plucked from the thistle and discarded after the soft end is nibbled. Cold asparagus can be held between the fingers and eaten whole or sliced and eaten with a fork. Shrimp may be peeled and the shells discarded; shrimp cocktail is eaten with a small fork and the tails are discarded. At a formal dinner, watch your hostess for cues.

One dish that everyone has tried and some have difficulty with is *spaghetti*! Today we will be having spaghetti noodles. We will be serving on your left side, so please lean a bit to the right when the food comes to your plate. Keep your good posture throughout the meal.

Please wait for everyone to be served. Once everyone is served, I will show you the proper way to eat long pasta noodles. Always wait before you begin a meal. This is part of good table manners. Here are some other tips on dining.

Once your host or hostess has welcomed you and everyone has had a chance to meet and then be seated, someone will probably call for your attention. (This is often done by lightly tapping the edge of a goblet with the tip of a knife.) Everyone should stop what they are doing and sit at attention. Someone will probably thank you all for coming and give thanks for the meal. This is often called "Grace" "Invocation," or the "Blessing." It can be short and sweet or quite lengthy. In any case, you must sit quietly, with hands folded in reverence for the duration of the words offered. Show respect for your host and hostess whenever they speak. Before you eat, wait until the hostess has put her napkin on her lap and taken the first bite.

If someone asks you to pass the salt, give him or her the salt and pepper. They go together. If there is no salt on the table, that probably means the meal has been salted. It would be impolite to ask for more salt. Taste every dish; you may discover a new favorite food. Don't take more food than you can finish, and wait to be excused when the host and hostess stand to leave. Always thank the hostess for inviting you and compliment her on the meal or the part you enjoyed most.

Now, let's get on with our specific lesson and dish of the day. You'll receive breadsticks on your bread plate. These don't require butter. They can be used to soak up sauce, or as a pusher. To stay neat, we aren't having sauce with the noodles. However, you may have grated cheese if you like.

Here is the proper way to eat long pasta noodles: roll a few strands at a time onto the tip of your fork. Some hosts and hostesses provide a large spoon to help you. You'll find it placed above or to the right of the dinner plate. Hold it in the left hand with the fork in the right hand, or you may use the side of your plate to help roll the noodles. Shorter strands can be gathered with the tip of the fork and eaten. Please do not slurp noodles into your mouth, whipping sauce in every direction! Bite off trailing ends and return them to your plate with the fork. This takes practice, but it can be done.

Another dining tip: Sometimes pasta sauce contains bay leaves, seeds, or sausage. If you find something like this that doesn't feel right in your mouth, here's how to remove it: first, try to eat any of it that you can and then remove it with your spoon and place it on the edge of your plate. If it happens to be an unsightly piece of gristle or bone, silently and discreetly spit it into the corner of your napkin, then keep it folded in the napkin on your lap until you go or request a new napkin.

A big part of your responsibility as a guest is to share conversations with the other guests at your table. Customarily, conversation moves around the table to the right. However, you should also occasionally speak to the person on your left and to the person across from you. Try to include people in the conversation by asking questions such as, "What did you think of that?" or "How did you feel about that?" This will allow you to listen to them speak about themselves. People like to talk about themselves and someone who will listen is considered charming. Take care not to dominate the conversation or one person's attention. Take turns listening.

It is easier to eat while listening than while you are speaking, and you must never speak with food in your mouth! If you notice that someone hasn't been able to stop talking long enough to eat, say something to carry the conversation for a minute or change the subject and give the person a break. Everyone should dine at about the same pace, so various courses of the meal can be prepared and put on the table together. It is a team effort between the diners, the servers, and the kitchen to have everything stay on schedule.

Never say or do anything *offensive* at the table. This includes vulgar language, rude or animalistic behavior, descriptions of wounds, illnesses, surgeries or accidents, etc. These subjects tend to put people off and make them lose their appetites. This would be an insult to your host and hostess, because they want everyone to enjoy the meal they have so thoughtfully provided.

Other conversation taboos include politics and religion. These are very personal subjects about which people tend to become emotional—even passionate. At a formal dining affair people are expected to control emotions and behave as ladies and gentlemen. Your dining table should stay on a fairly even keel— steady as she goes as a big ship at sea. Don't "rock the boat." Controversial subjects will not be welcome and should be left at the door. Part of the reality of Etiquette Lessons is that we have 0-tolerance for bad language and disruptive behavior. Offenders will be dismissed.

Let's talk about personality. Say we are at a dinner party and Snow White is our hostess. Who do we have sitting at the table with us? Give me several names please. Who would you be? Of course we would have to include Grumpy, Bashful, Sleepy, Happy and who else? Now that we have our tablemates with a variety of personalities, let's have a conversation. This ball will represent our conversation, and we will toss it around when we address each other. When attending a dinner party, you must come prepared. Remember to bring at least one joke, a compliment, an article of news, check the weather, and know current events like the score of the latest "big game." We'll start with Miss or Mr. Happy. What do you do first when you want to speak to someone? How do you properly address someone at the dinner table? Yes, you call them by name and what else? You call them by their name and *title*, yes. Then and only then do you have their attention and the attention of others who will want to hear his answer. Now you can toss them the ball and ask a question. They in turn will toss the ball back and answer, or hold the ball while answering you, then call someone else's name and toss the ball to them with a new question. For example, "Miss or Mr. Happy, (toss the ball) how did you meet our hostess, Miss Snow White?"

"I met her at a garden party last summer."

"Mr. Grumpy, (toss) how did you meet Miss Snow White?"

We'll take turns until every one has shared in the conversation. You see, no matter what their personalities are like, each dinner guest is expected to engage in conversation.

Try not to "drop the ball" by not answering a question. Remember, we are indoors and using the ball as a symbol for conversation. Please pay attention to what we are doing; be quiet and keep the conversation going.

Once in a blue moon (not very often) you may be given a fingerbowl before dessert. It will be placed in front of you as a small bowl with a doily under it on a dessert plate, a dessert fork on the plate beside the bowl on the left, and a teaspoon on the plate to the right of the bowl. Using both hands, pick up the finger bowl and doily and place them on the table to the upper left of your dessert plate for later use. Place the utensils on the table. Dessert will be served on your plate. Eat the dessert with your spoon in the right hand, using the fork in your left as a pusher. When finished, place the fork and spoon on the plate for removal. Lastly, pick up the finger bowl and doily and place them in front of you. Dip fingertips of each hand in turn into the bowl and dry them with your napkin. Place the napkin in loose folds on the left as you leave the table.

(Lesson 3—Quiz Time)

That completes the lesson for today.

Girls and Boys at the Table: Lesson Three

Quiz

Questions and Answers

Question 1. **T/F)** Cooked, chilled asparagus may be eaten with the fingers.

Answer: True, unless it is in a sauce like Hollandaise.

Question 2. **T/F)** Salt and pepper are passed together as a set.

Answer: True, even if someone just asks for salt.

Question 3. Do breadsticks require butter?

Answer: No, they do not, but in some homes it is done.

Question 4. Before making an announcement or a toast, what is the proper way to get everyone's attention?

Answer: Very lightly, tap the top edge of your goblet with the tip of the back of your dinner knife.

Question 5. What subjects are not appropriate for dinner conversation?

Answer: Never say or do anything offensive during dinner. This includes vulgar language, rude or animalistic behavior, descriptions of wounds, illnesses, surgeries or accidents, etc. Other conversation taboos include politics and religion.

Girls & Boys at the Table

Lesson 4: Bow, Curtsey, Handshake, Reception Lines, Introductions, Invitations & Thank You Notes

Hello everyone. We will begin with a bit of protocol instruction. Who can define the word "protocol," as in "computer protocol "? The term, "computer protocol" is a set of rules that govern the format of messages exchanged between computers.

Likewise, for us humans, "protocol" means the rules about how to meet someone properly in a social setting. In this lesson, we are dealing with some of the protocol of basic "Introductions." We will talk about the handshake, bow and curtsey. As soon as everyone has washed their hands or used hand sanitizer, we will begin. Please form a line or two here, facing me.

Say you have just given a performance or received an award at a school assembly. Everyone is applauding. It is appropriate for you to hesitate, take a bow or curtsey to acknowledge and thank the audience before leaving the stage. It will also signal the audience that they can stop applauding.

Girls, this is how to curtsey: lightly lift both sides of your skirt, or if you are wearing slacks, raise your arms out to the sides to keep your balance. In one smooth motion, shift your weight to the left leg, bend your knees, tap your right toe behind you, lower your eyes and nod your head. The deeper the curtsey, the more reverence and appreciation is conveyed. Sometimes you may even want to place your hand over your heart during a curtsey. When being introduced on stage, you may curtsey but keep your chin up. Maintain eye contact so the audience can see your face. All the girls, please try a curtsey together. Thank you. That looks very nice.

Now, boys, a bow is taken from the waist with knees straight and a nod of the head, either with your hands at your sides or more formally, with your hands behind you or with your right hand over your heart and your left hand behind you. Boys, altogether, please take a bow. Thank you.

Please note: we live in a society where direct eye contact is expected and welcomed as a positive form of communication. Everyone should remember to use eye contact often.

When you are introducing two people to each other, you should name the person of higher rank or age first. For example, "Grandmother, this is my teacher, Mr. Scott." Or, "Mr. Scott, this is my friend, Nick." Remember to use a title when introducing adults: Mr., Mrs., Ms., Dr., etc. This is a way of showing respect. Ask people if they have a personal preference in how you address them on a regular basis. (Being on a "First Name" basis should be considered a privilege.)

When you are introducing someone to a group, make a gesture toward that person, telling a little something about him or her to queue the conversation. For example, "I would like you all to meet my cousin Baron, who just flew in from Atlanta."

"Air kisses" and other greetings may come and go, but normally a handshake is expected when you meet both ladies and gentlemen, especially in a business setting. This is how a proper handshake is done: With your right hand, firmly grasp the other person's right hand, palm to palm. Together, pump your hands once and release. Again, your hands will come together, rise up, down, and up again with the release. Let's try it. Walk past me on the way to find your seats, stopping to give me your handshake.

Please find your seat and stand behind it. Before you are seated, gentlemen, remember to offer to help the ladies with their chairs.

Next, you will each pretend that you are planning to have a party. Let's say it is your Birthday Party. We must write the invitations, and since we should expect to receive a few gifts, we shall also practice composing thank you notes. We won't need place settings today because we will be having finger foods and appetizers, and they will be served after we do some writing. For that you will find an index card and something to write with on your placemat.

You will receive your beverage now. Beverages are served from the right; lean a little to the left to be out of the way. Hold the cup for the pourer, please. In a formal dining room your waiter will usually pick up your goblet, the fill and return it to the upper right of your place setting. He will also remove any wine glasses you will obviously not need.

Until now we have been learning general good manners and the etiquette of being a good dinner guest. Today we will discuss the etiquette of hosting. When you give a party, *you* are the host or hostess, and that means you have certain responsibilities to your guests. First of all, you need to send them an invitation. We must make sure they know the "four W's" of our event. What are the four W's?

Raise your hand if you can tell me the first of the four W's. The first is *Who*—who is the birthday party for? You, of course, so write the word "Who:" and then write your name.

Now we need the other three W's. Who can tell me the second W? That's right, it's *What*—meaning what kind of party? Now write *What?* and then "Birthday Party" on the same line.

Our guests will know we are having a birthday party. What else do they need to know? What are the third and fourth W's?

Who knows the third? Newspaper articles have the four W's. Yes! *When* is next. We must inform our guests when the party will be. That includes the date and the time. On the third line write, "When:" and then write your date and time. For example: Saturday, November 8, 2:30–5:30 PM.

Who knows what to write on the last line? Yes, *Where?* Our guests need to know where the party will be held. On the fourth line of your invitation, write "Where:" and the location of your party.

Written in this order on your invitation:

The Four W's of Invitations are:
WHO: Whose party is it?
WHAT: What is the occasion?
WHEN: When is the party?
WHERE: Where is the party?

Can you think of anything else that should go on the invitation? The guests need more information. A proper invitation has additional information in the lower left and the lower right corners.

I'll give you a hint; it has to do with your guest's responsibilities. Yes, they must know how to let you know if they plan to attend your party. They must give you a response. How can they do this? Invitation protocol requires that you provide them with—what? Yes, RSVP. They need a phone number and the name of someone who is waiting to hear their response. In the lower left corner of our invitation we write the letters RSVP, followed by a phone number. You should also give them the date by which you need to know how many guests are coming and the name of someone who is waiting for their call. Who knows the meaning of the term "RSVP?" Of course, it means, "Respond, if you please," or in the original French, *Repondez-vous s'il vous plait.*

Now you will be served appetizers. Please eat quietly while the lesson continues. A word about the food: These appetizers are made especially for Etiquette Lesson students; they are called "Funny Face Finger Food." The faces are made of cheese and celery, baby carrots, Spanish olives, salami, crackers and a pickle. Try it; I think you'll like it.

The discussion of RSVP gives us an opportunity to practice telephone etiquette. I have two telephones to practice with. We'll take turns confirming that we will or cannot attend someone's party. When I make the sound of a phone ringing, you will answer using proper telephone etiquette and say,

"Hello, _____ residence, _____speaking." Then the other student will tell you the reason for the call, saying first, "Hello, this is_____calling, may I speak to_____?

(Ask your parents for family rules on telephone safety. What do they want you to tell people who call for them when they are not at home? I suggest you say, "They are busy; may I have them call you back?" Take simple messages of name and telephone number; details can be very confusing.)

A very formal affair like a wedding will often require an invitation with a response card included with a stamped envelope for return post. Guests can simply mark the card and send it back with their intentions. This saves guests from making long distance phone calls and allows a third person—like a wedding planner, for example—to manage the guest list. Some invitations include maps to an event. If guests are traveling some distance, the formal invitation might include nearby hotel and restaurant information as well.

What information about our party should we provide in the lower right corner of our invitation? What else does your guest need to know? Does the party have a theme? Is it, for example, a swimming party? If so, your guests should be prepared to bring their swim wear. That's right, it is the host or hostess's responsibility to advise quests of what to wear to his or her party. You want your guests to dress appropriately so they will feel at ease and not be over-dressed or under-dressed. Attire notes go in the lower right corner on your invitation.

I'll come around and check your work. Your birthday party invitation should have the four W's, the RSVP, and attire notes.

(For those in the younger grades, it is sufficient to write only four W's, on four lines, **"RSVP"** on the lower left and **"Attire"** on the lower right on your card. Those who aren't writing yet can just put down four big "W's", the letters RSVP on the left, and a drawing of an appropriate article of clothing on the right.) Now, let's say the party was a big success and our guests have given us something for our birthday. What do you think they might have given us? That's right: gifts! Please turn your invitations over because now we will write a *Thank you Note* on the back of the card.

A Thank You Note should be short, sweet, and personal. The proper Thank you note covers 5 points: **1.)** Say the person's name in your greeting. **2.)** Name the actual gift they gave you. **3.)** Say what you like about it. **4.)** Thank them for coming to your party. **5.)** Use a friendly closing like, "Your friend,_____" and sign your first name in ink. It should be delivered within three days from the time the gift is received. Keep a list of the gifts and who brought them so you won't get confused. For example:

Dear Molly,
Thank you for the friendship bracelet,
I will wear it everyday!
Thank you for coming to my birthday party.
    Your friend,
    Phoebe

Try to write a thank you note that will bring a smile to the face of the person who receives it when they read it, just as their gift brought a smile to your face when you opened it.

Write the note, pretending that the gift was from the person across the table from you. Make something up; be creative. Do the best job that you can; say something specific about why you like the gift. We'll take turns reading them aloud.

(Lesson 4—Quiz Time)

We will end Lesson 4 with the presentation of your Etiquette Certificates. Please form a line at the front of the room. Congratulations!

Girls and Boys at the Table Lesson Four

Quiz

Questions and Answers

Question 1.) What are the 4 W's of a proper Invitation?
Answer: Who, What, When and Where.

Question 2.) Define the word "Protocol."
Answer: Protocol is a set of rules that govern meetings.

Question 3.) When introducing a lady & gentleman, whose name do you say first?
Answer: Say the lady's name first, as "Ms. Jennifer, I'd like you to meet Mr. Robert." You are presenting him to her.

Question 4.) Which hand do we shake hands with?
Answer: We always shake hands with the right hand.

Question 5.) What are the 5 points of a proper Thank You Note?
Answer: 1.) Write the person's name, of course.
2.) Name the actual gift.
3.) Tell something you like about it.
4.) Thank them for coming to your party.
5.) End the note in a friendly way, signing your first name in ink.

Etiquette Lessons

Teens at the Table

Parts I and II

A Word to the Teens

In ancient times, only royals were taught the rules of etiquette. In fact, the word "etiquette" in 14th century royal courts meant "a ticket," in reference to an invitation or special pass required to be in the company of the king and queen.

In America, we are all free to learn the rules of etiquette and be on our best behavior everywhere. We are free to enter high society at any time. A place in society is not just something you are born into or buy; it is a way of life, which you prepare for and achieve.

Etiquette lessons apply to any social situation, from sitting around the dinner table at home with family to lunch with classmates or to the most formal affairs with heads of State. The content of these lessons is about the intelligent presentation of yourself and a reciprocal exchange with others.

Be prepared to make a rather solemn commitment: *the promise to conform.* Put aside rude behavior and be trained in the social graces. (For example, personal presentation must hold to traditional standards, rather than yield to popular fashion.) The lessons here are rules of the game for meeting and interacting with others. Formal social occasions are like playing fields, with many rules for everyone. Keep an open mind, learn the skills, cloak yourself in humility, and take this opportunity to practice how to behave well.

Yes, practice is required so doing things the proper way becomes automatic, and old, bad habits are forgotten. Later, when you enter society and all physical standards have been met, you have passed protocol and have been seated, your only real challenge will be what to say. Once that is perceived as an opportunity rather than a challenge, use your table manners and work toward perfecting the art of conversation. You will navigate the stream of dining conversation with many fascinating companions. The goal of society is advancement for each person—advancement for society as a whole and even for the entire human race! This is done through the peaceful exchange of thoughts and ideas, usually shared over a meal.

You won't be *eating* anymore; you will *dine*. Take dining etiquette seriously. Your good behavior will assure others that you come in peace. Let it be the guide to your social survival. Charm adults with your personal knowledge of how things are done. Impress others with courtesy, self-confidence and good conversation. Practice, and this will become natural to you. Our culture and way of life survive within these time-honored traditions which are practiced currently by four generations of ladies and gentlemen. Now it is your turn to embrace tradition, use it, refine it, and preserve it for future generations. Our first lesson will be on Table Manners.

Teens at the Table

Lesson Guide

(A Must Read for Instructors)

Welcome to *Teens at the Table* Etiquette Lessons! These lessons were designed for classes of 12 to 24 students, with a time allotment of 45 minutes each. Lessons contain a lecture and a demonstration, writing and drawing activities, food service, eating, and clearing tables. Lessons are written in scripts for the instructor to read while students work through activities in three 15-minute segments per lesson, one lesson per class. It is appropriate for students in middle school and high school. (Instructors will need assistance serving more than 12 students.) Before class begins, place tableware on a side table and put a placemat at each student's seat. Each lesson includes a healthy snack, prepared beforehand and served in the later part of the class, after the table is set or written activities are completed. Food should be kept fresh or warm and out of sight until served. Always serve food from the left and remove dishes from the right. For best results, the instructor and assistants should look formal by wearing a white blouse or shirt with a black skirt or slacks or a basic black or dark dress with pearl accessories.

Furniture Required

Students may use their own desktop at school or sit at a cafeteria table, picnic bench, or dining table. As described above, the instructor will also need a table for the display of dishes, flatware, cups, napkins, and a staging area for food, with a refrigerator nearby.

Supplies Needed

The instructor will read Lesson Scripts in this book, Instructor will need: one serving tray, tongs, a ladle, a pitcher, a breadbasket for each 12 students, and a ball to toss. Optional: a punch bowl. A white board and two telephone headsets are helpful.

Students will need plain white napkins, paper place mats, paper plates and desert plates (to be used as bread plates), doilies for desert plates, plastic cups, bowls for soup, plastic knives, forks and spoons, 3X5" index cards, and pens or pencils.

Teens at the Table Part I, *Table Manners and Good Behavior* This Part establishes the basic foundation in etiquette lessons needed upon which to build Part II. Teens at the Table, Part I, is similar to "Girls & Boys at the Table," but contains age-appropriate terms, subjects, language and menu items for teens.

Part II, Lessons 5,6,7 and 8 make up the "American Cotillion Lessons." These are to be considered advanced etiquette lessons. They focus more closely on formal dining, specific foods, attire, hygiene and behavior. In these lessons we introduce the seven-course banquet and practice Ball Room Dancing. Proper ambience calls for white tablecloths and cloth napkins, with vases of cut flowers on the table. Slipcovers may be used on folding chairs. Paper and plastic supplies will suffice, but use silver and china when your budget and logistics allow. The instructor will need a CD player and the following certain classic recordings. Dance shoes or street shoes are recommended over sport shoes.

Music and Dance

For the Beginning Slow Dance in Lesson six, we use "<u>Born Free</u>" by John Barry and Roger Williams. For the Waltz, also in Lesson Seven, we use Johann Strauss Jr.'s, "<u>On the Beautiful Blue Danube</u>" and "<u>Yesterday</u>" by Lennon and McCartney. For transition from Waltz to Rumba and Cha-Cha—the first Latin beats appearing in the Ballroom in Lesson Eight—we use, "<u>The Girl from Ipanema</u>" by Stan Getz and Astrud Gilberto. Then Mr. Glenn Miller's most famous song, "<u>In the Mood</u>" introduces fun, upbeat Swing Dancing, followed by basic Rock and Roll with "<u>Rockin' Robin</u>" by Bobby Day. These songs have been carefully chosen for the easy-to-follow beat and simple lyrics. Recordings of these classics can be found in department store music aisles, libraries, or private collections.

Teens at the Table: Part I
Table Manners and Social Behavior Lessons
Course Content and Food Service Per Lesson

Lesson One

Virtual Dining Room Serve melon, such as cantaloupe, honeydew or watermelon, sliced in crescent or wedge shapes approximately 1/2 inch thick. Students may have second servings. Serve, with tongs, one at a time. These are used to practice proper use of the fork and knife for slicing and eating bite-sized pieces of steak or turkey. Also serve graham crackers on the bread plate, and lemonade or apple juice. Note: In Lesson One, focus is on the *place setting*. The instructor should use this opportunity to observe the students' eating habits and briefly introduce proper use of the knife and fork.

Lesson Two

Advanced Dining Etiquette This lesson calls for dinner rolls, fresh and warm from the oven if possible, served from a basket with tongs. Provide enough so that each student may have several rolls. Place them one at a time on the bread plate. Also serve butter in balls or pats on a dish, and lemonade or apple juice.

Lesson Three

Best Guest Dinner Conversation As part of the discussion of difficult foods to eat, serve buttered spaghetti noodles with grated parmesan cheese, short breadsticks, lemonade, apple juice or white grape juice, anda ball for tossing in the conversation lesson.

Lesson Four

Host with the Most Social Correspondence This is basically a writing lesson and does not require a place setting. You will need placemats, index cards, and pens or pencils. During the last 15 minutes, serve a small plate of appetizers such as caviar, pate, smoked oysters, brie, stuffed mushrooms, etc., along with ice water. Use 6" desert plates with doilies.

Teens at the Table Part II
The American Cotillion Lessons
Course Content and Food Service Per Lesson

Lesson Five

Fine Dining Vocabulary. Serve cold potato soup (Vichyssoise), with dinner rolls or "Pop-overs" fresh and warm from the oven with strawberry soup, water or juice. This lesson is used to introduce banquet-style, seven-course meals which begin with a soup course. At every opportunity we strive to offer samplings of delicacies to educate the palate, and instruction on how to eat them. Instructors, use the resources at hand; your choices may vary.

Lesson Six

Conversation and Communication. Serve melon, such as cantaloupe, honeydew or watermelon, sliced in crescent or wedge shapes approximately 1/2 inch thick. Students may have second servings. Serve with tongs, one slice at a time. These are used to practice the proper use of the fork and knife for slicing and eating bite-sized pieces of steak or turkey. Also serve lavosh or assorted crackers on the bread plate. Students serve themselves or each other from a punch bowl. Students learn the basic ballroom dance holding position.

Lesson Seven

Dressing For Dinner. Serve Italian Ice, Glaces or light sorbets with flavored water and sweet crackers to clear the palate after the heavier meat courses. A light repast allows more time for discussion of proper hygiene and formal attire, American Ballroom History, and to practice dances, beginning with the slow dance and the waltz.

Lesson Eight

Dance Floor Etiquette. Dancing at a banquet would begin with the sixth, or dessert course. You may serve desserts such as cake and ice cream on dessert plates, and punch or lemonade. Dancing continues with the seventh course (coffee course), for which we substitute a fare of chocolate milk, mixed nuts, bonbons or brownies instead of coffee. Lesson Eight begins with a presentation of the students and their certificates and awards. We practice the receiving line, escorting, being seated, etc. More music and dance styles are introduced. Students may wish to dress up for this occasion. Suggested attire would include shirts with collars and slacks for boys, dresses or skirts for girls.

Although Part II is an American Cotillion course and would logically end with a sixth or seventh course menu, instructors may choose to complete the Etiquette Program with the grand tradition of High Tea. When this is done, we call it a "Teen Tea-Dance." See instructions below. Also, here are some recipes you will need. For best results, have these prepared fresh just before class. Teens at the Table snacks should always be prepared and presented with pride, enjoyed, and savored with appreciation. This and good conversation are the essence of fine and formal dining.

Food Service for Teen Tea Dance

High Tea is served in three courses. Students make selections from trays or 3-tiered desert platters. Arrange on a tray from the outside to the center, or from bottom to top. The first course will be finger sandwiches, enough of three types for each student to try one of each: two made of meat spreads such as turkey, ham, chicken, beef and tuna. The third variety of sandwich offered should be a sandwich of thinly sliced cucumbers with cream cheese. Use white bread, cut off the crusts and cut sandwiches into triangle-shaped fourths. The second course is scones (see scone recipe below). Provide one large scone or two small scones for each student. Scones are traditionally served with clotted (over-whipped) cream and strawberry preserves served in bowls. The third course is petit fours, truffles, chocolates or other delights—approximately two each. Supplies required for High Tea include a dessert dish with a napkin, knife, fork, spoon and cup. Serve flavored ice teas.

Elsie's Scones

3 1/2 cups unbleached all-purpose flour
5 teaspoons baking powder
6 tablespoons sugar
1/2 teaspoon fine salt
12 tablespoons unsalted butter, cut into 1/2 inch cubes and refrigerated
1/2 cup diced raisins, dried currants or dried cranberries 2 large eggs
2/3 cup heavy cream 1 cup sugar (set aside)

Preheat oven to 425 degrees E Yield: 12 scones

Sift together the flour, baking powder, sugar and salt. Add butter and blend into a crumbly texture. Stir in dried fruit.

In a separate bowl, beat eggs and cream together, then add to flour mixture until workable. On floured surface, knead dough into three equal balls. Cut each ball of dough into four wedges. Roll the scones in sugar and space evenly on baking sheet until golden edged, about 12 to 15 minutes.

Ella's PopOvers

1 cup all-purpose flour
1/2 teaspoon salt
1 cup 1% low fat milk
2 large eggs

1 tablespoon butter, melted
Cooking spray
1 teaspoon vegetable oil

1.) Preheat oven to 375 degrees

2.) Lightly spoon flour into a dry measuring cup, level with a knife. Combine flour and salt, stirring with a whisk. Combine milk and eggs in a medium bowl, stirring with a whisk until blended; let stand 30 minutes to remove the chill from eggs and milk. Gradually add flour mixture, stirring well with a whisk. Stir in butter.

3.) Pre-warm the popover cups or muffin tins. Brush or spray with oil to coat cups. Divide and fill batter evenly among prepared popover cups. Bake at 375 for 40 minutes or until "popped" and golden. Serve immediately with soup or salad. Please do not open the oven door to peek, for they shall fail to pop!

Estella's Strawberry Soup

24 Big, fresh, strawberries
1 quart of skim milk

1 gal. strawberry ice cream
8 oz. strawberry cream cheese spread

1.) Clean, slice and chop strawberries in blender.

2.) Add skim milk to strawberries and liquefy.

3.) Blend ice cream into berries and milk mixture.

4.) Fold and then blend in cream cheese spread. This secret ingredient binds the flavors and gives body to the soup.

Transport Strawberry Soup in a lidded plastic pitcher. Pour into bowls. Makes approx. 2 gallons of soup. Keep chilled and serve as soon as possible.

Evelyn's Cranberry Punch

One Gal. cranberry juice	One 2-liter bottle Canada Dry Ginger Ale
Pint pineapple sherbet	1 cup fresh cranberries

Combine the first three ingredients together and chill. Garnish with fresh cranberries and orange slices. Makes about 26 servings.

Teens at the Table

Part I
Table Manners and
Good Social Behavior

Teens at the Table

Part I
Table Manners and
Good Social Behavior

Lesson 1: Virtual Dining Room

Welcome to the class. Now that we are here, please be quiet and listen. Etiquette Class is a virtual, formal dining room. In a formal dining room, the mood is serene. This is *Silence is Golden.* Guests enjoy live chamber music or classical recordings played quietly. When someone does speak, everyone politely listens. Servers speak in whispers or not at all. When someone speaks in a formal dining room, they speak because they have something to say. Bad language is forbidden. Please be quiet and keep the virtual dining room in mind. We are here for intelligent exchange. We have a lot of material to cover in very little time, so let's get started.

Again, welcome to the class, I am_____. Let's start by getting to know each other. *Pay close attention during introductions, because next we are going to play a memory game!*

Everyone has a title such as Mrs., Mr., Miss or Ms. Remember to use titles when addressing or introducing adults. This is a way to show respect. Titles acknowledge an adult person's maturity and accomplishments. At social gatherings where we expect to meet new people, the first step, of course, is the name exchange.

In a formal social setting we would start with our title first, and then use our first and last name or surname. The titles *Miss* and *Mister* are used for young ladies and gentlemen like you. *Master* is used for posting letters to young men who may share the same name with their father. Titles help define who we are, while at the same time protecting our privacy.

If this were a formal occasion, you would be introduced with Miss or Mr. before your first and last names. It is a privilege to be introduced to someone and to be on a first-name basis. First names and nicknames are usually shared only with close family members and friends at school. A good host and hostess will make an effort to introduce all of their guests to each other so that when the music begins ladies and gentlemen will feel more comfortable dancing together because they have already been introduced.

Getting back to introducing ourselves, if you know each other already, we won't use your first names or surnames. What is left? How shall we introduce ourselves? That's right, we will use *middle* names to make it seem like we are meeting someone new. Please fold the index card in front of you horizontally and write your middle name on it. There should also be a pen or pencil there. Next we will take turns introducing ourselves by middle names. Here's a tip: when you hear someone's name for the first time, associate it with an object the name and the person remind you of. Use familiar objects like those you would find around the table, in the garage, or in the garden. This will help you remember. Be sure to use positive images, because our minds tend to forget negative things. Has everyone finished writing? Please put your pens down and pass your index cards to me. We'll start with the middle name introductions. What is your middle name? And yours? etc.

Now, here's how we play the game. I will choose someone; they have to tell me their name and the name of the person to their right and the person to their left, then call the name of someone else who will do the same, until everyone has had a turn.

When you choose someone, say their name and nod to them; remember it is not polite to point. If you don't know them, just nod when you have eye contact. I will start the memory game with *you*. Please give me your name and the names of your neighbors.

We always try to learn the names of the other people with whom we are dining. There are several reasons for this. Can anyone guess what they are? Yes, to be sociable, or in business we call it "networking." We also remember names so if we need something at the table that is not in front of us and there is no waiter, we can ask for it using the name of the person closest to it. For example, "Kevin, please pass the butter." We ask others to pass things to us because it is considered rude to lean over the table or reach across in front of someone.

A gentleman should address a young lady by name when he asks her to dance. If he doesn't know her name, he should strive to get an introduction before he asks for a dance. Young ladies prefer to dance with gentlemen to whom they have been introduced.

What are the magic words to use when asking for and receiving something? *Please* and *Thank you* of course. If someone says *Thank you* to you, how should you respond? That's right, *You're welcome*. You know some of this already.

Our lesson for today is about *place settings*. Place settings define our personal space when we sit down to eat at the table. You will each learn to set your place at the table. Place settings can have a few pieces and be very simple for casual dining, or they can have a lot of pieces and be very fancy for formal dining. How many of you help set the table at home?

Families often sit at the table together for meals. While at the table together we have time to tell each other stories about our busy days, plan activities or discuss news. At the family dinner table we can talk things over, ask questions, and make announcements where everyone takes turns speaking and listening. This is a forum where parents teach family values. Training in dining etiquette begins at home. "Teens at the Table" graduates practice good etiquette at home so good manners will become natural.

Unfortunately, we all have busy schedules these days and many of our meals are eaten "on the run." Meals are sometimes picked up at the drive-through window and eaten with our hands in the car, picnic style. Finger food is very popular these days. How many eat pizza at least twice a month? It's true; most of us eat at least one meal with our hands each day.

I know that talking about food makes us hungry. Don't worry, we will have a little snack soon. So why do we have to learn good table manners and etiquette? Who can tell me why we study etiquette? Because many rules of dining etiquette can go anywhere, even with fast food. For example, "Don't speak with your mouth full" and "Put your napkin on your lap."

The really great thing about etiquette is that it is the *equalizer*. It is by means of the same etiquette you are learning here today in our virtual formal dining room that you can sit down with anyone in America from any ethnic background and share a meaningful exchange. In fact, Heads of State use these same rules in foreign diplomatic functions.

We also study etiquette because we sometimes attend formal dining occasions—like Thanksgiving dinner, or wedding receptions—in fine restaurants and dining rooms where we must know how to feed ourselves with flatware and behave properly. Who can tell me what flatware is?

Flatware, silverware, or cutlery refers to the knife, fork, and spoon you use to eat. The basic formal *Place Setting* has 6 parts. Their position on the table in front of you is very important. They are your tools for dining properly. Here is a rhyme to help you remember them:

The Place Setting Rhyme

Hey Diddle Diddle,

My plate in the Middle,

And we'll be eating soon.

My fork on the Left,

Below the bread plate,

Across from my cup and spoon.

My knife on the Right,

Its blade facing in,

And now we can begin.

TKGR

We have the plates, cups, and everything else we need to make a place setting. First we will draw a picture of the rhyme so we know where everything goes in our Place Setting.

What comes first? Yes, the plate, so draw a circle the size of your plate. Then where does the fork go? Think of the rhyme again. Yes on the left, below what? The bread plate, is always on your left with the fork. So draw a fork and a smaller circle representing the bread plate above it on the left side of the plate.

What is across from the bread plate and fork? Ah, the cup and spoon, which go on the right. Draw a small circle for the cup, and below it draw a spoon. What else is on the right? Yes, the knife. The knife lies between the plate and the spoon at the right of the plate. Who can tell me which way the blade should face and why? Yes, it's facing the food, ready for use.

Say the rhyme again; memorize it. Say it at home. Practice setting the table at home when you can. Now we will put all the place setting pieces on our pictures. When it is your turn, please quietly go to the plate table and find what you need, come back and put them—one piece at a time—on your picture.

Once our places are set we can have a little refreshment. For that we need something to protect our clothes from spills and crumbs falling into our lap. What do we need? Yes, that's right. A napkin, sometimes called a "serviette," is usually found to the left of your plate under the fork. However, some hosts and hostesses like to break away from tradition with the placement of napkins. You will often find the table in a formal dining room set with the dinner or luncheon napkin placed in your empty beverage glass (on the right side of the plate, of course). It may be folded and placed in the coffee cup in front of you or folded into the shape of a bird of paradise and sitting in the center of your dinner plate. When you sit down at the table, one of the first things to do is to place your napkin on your lap. If your hostess is at the table with you, do so when she does. Open a cloth dinner napkin halfway with the fold toward you, a square luncheon napkin opens completely. If you must leave the table during a meal, place your napkin on the seat of your chair, not on the table. When you are done eating, pick up your napkin loosely and place it on the table to the left of your plate.

As the rhyme says, "Now we can begin." We are serving melon with today's lesson. Use the melon to practice your cutting and eating skills. All meats, such as steak, turkey, and fish, should be cut and eaten one bite at a time. Your knife and fork are used as extensions of your pointer fingers. Hold your fork without making a fist. Use your fork to hold the meat in place while slicing it with your knife in a stroking motion. We are not sawing wood.

There have been two traditional styles of cutting and eating with a knife and fork. These are known as the Continental Style, which is slicing and eating with both knife and fork in one process and American Style, slicing in one process using both knife and fork, putting the knife down and transferring the fork into the right hand, then conveying of sliced meat and all other items in a second process with the fork only. Both are perfectly acceptable ways to dine and they work well together.

("Etiquette Lessons" author, Teresa Grisinger Reilly, is in agreement with Victorian-American, etiquette authority, Emily Post, that the Continental style is the preferred slicing process. However, Mrs. Reilly, notes that a modern diet with more emphasis on vegetables, fruits and grains requires less slicing, and meals are eaten more quickly. She suggests a more appropriate and natural style of dining can be achieved by alternating the Continental and the American style. She has therefore coined the term, "Concert Style." Concert Style dining combines the more quiet Continental style with the quick American style in consideration of today's faster paced meals and softer diet.)

The following is an example of Concert Style Dining: Begin in the Continental Style by slicing off a piece of melon and keeping the fork in your left hand with the bite of melon on it, simply pop that bite into your mouth. Still holding the knife in your right hand and fork in your left hand, rest your wrists on the table edge while chewing or talking. Proceed with cutting off another piece. this styles is appropriate when you want to make take several bites in succession, cut and eat one at a time. At a meal, with the tip of your knife, a bit of vegetables or potato could be placed on the back of your down-turned fork, on top of your bite of meat before it goes into your mouth. Looking down you should be able to see the top of your hands, with your pointer fingers extended on top of the knife and fork. When you are taking a break while dining, place your knife and fork (prongs down) in the shape of an "X" on your plate. This means, "At Rest." or "X" Marks the spot, do not remove my treasure!"

Continue in the American Style by slicing off a new piece of melon. Then put the knife down at the top edge of the plate with its blade facing in and place the fork with the bite of melon on it into your right hand. Your left hand may rest in your lap. Eat that bite and then use the fork to pick up another item on your plate and eat that. Finally, lay the fork down on the left side of the plate, sip your beverage and chat for a while. Your knife and fork await your next procedure. You may want to use both hands to take something from your bread plate now. When you are ready to slice again, use the Continental style or the American style depending on how many bites you want in a series. If your entre is a soft meat, you may be able to cut it with the side of your fork, keeping the fork in your right hand. Keep your bites small so you can participate conversation without speaking with food in your mouth. Stifle the urge to point with your knife or gesture with your fork as you speak.

To keep the tablecloth clean, do not place utensils back on the table once they have been used or lean them on the side of the plate like the oars on a rowboat. When finished, place both the knife and fork diagonally across your plate like the red international symbol for no on a no smoking sign. If the plate were a clock's face, the time would be ten minutes to four. This position tells your waiter to remove your plate. It means "Take it away." It also helps to keep the flatware from falling off when your plate is removed. When leaving your place at the table, replace your chair so it won't be in the way.

(Lesson 1—Quiz Time)

That completes our first lesson.

Teens at the Table Lesson One

Quiz

Questions and Answers

Question 1. What is the proper way to address an adult?
Answer: To show respect, children should address adults as "Ma'am" or "Sir" or use their surname (last name) with their title, like Ms., Mr., Dr. or Captain, etc.

Question 2. What are the three styles of dining?
Answer: There are two traditional styles of cutting and eating with a knife and fork. They are known as: "the American style" and "the Continental style." Both are perfectly acceptable and work nicely, "in concert" with one another. In fact, the combination of American and Continental styles of cutting and eating works best and may be considered a third style of eating called, "Concert Style"

Question 3. What is the "at rest" position for my utensils when I am not eating?

Answer: In the shape of an "X" across my plate, as if to say, "X marks the spot, this is my treasure, do not take it away."

Question 4. How do I show that I am finished eating?
Answer: I place the knife and fork diagonally across my plate from upper left to lower right. On a clock's face, this would be 10 minutes before four.

Question 5. Recite or write the Place Setting Rhyme.
Answer:

Place Setting Rhyme

Hey Diddle Diddle,
My plate in the Middle,
And we'll be eating soon.

My fork on the Left,
Below the bread plate,
Across from my cup and spoon.

My knife on the Right,
Its blade facing in,
And now we can begin.

TKGR

Teens at the Table

Part I
Table Manners and
Good Social Behavior

Lesson 2: Advanced Dining Etiquette

Welcome back; find your place at the table and we will begin. Today we are going to discuss things you can expect to happen before the meal is served in a formal dining room.

At formal dining occasions, you will find a card with your name on it where the hostess or people who planned the party want you to sit. It would be considered very rude to rearrange these cards. Seating alternates: boy, girl, boy, girl, etc. Why do you suppose that is done? This provides more opportunities for social interaction between boys and girls. With young people and single adults, this may be a way of meeting new friends. This is also done because society is generally made up of couples; we do tend to pair off eventually, and couples like to sit together.

By now you know that fine dining is much more than just eating. It is an elaborate ritual of sharing and celebrating important times together over a meal.

I should mention at this point that it is customary for a gentleman to help the lady on his right to be seated. First he asks, "May I help you?" She will respond by saying, "Yes, please." He proceeds by pulling her chair out from the table so she can step in front of it. She bends her knees as he gently pushes her chair under her while she sits down. Perhaps it is easier for a lady in a formal gown or beaded cocktail dress to sit with a little assistance. She will then say, "Thank you." We will practice this maneuver.

Everyone stand behind your chair. We'll start with you. Again, the gentleman takes the lady's chair by its back, saying, "May I help you?" She responds by saying "Yes, thank you." He first pulls her chair out. She steps in front of the chair. He then gently pushes her chair under her as she sits down. She starts to sit, putting one or both hands at her side, and then firmly holds the seat of the chair as it is scooted under her. When the gentleman lets go of the chair she can then finish pulling the chair under her while adjusting her distance from the table, saying, "Thank you." Then the gentleman seats himself. This maneuver requires communication and teamwork. Now you try it.

Here is a rhyme to help you remember good posture. Get plenty of sleep so that you do not need to prop yourselves up on elbows.

Mabel, Mabel, if you're able, Keep your elbows off the table.

As you know, good posture is important. Who can tell me why? We look better sitting up straight, we probably won't drop food on our chest, and our meal will digest better if our stomach is not crushed under our ribs, but given plenty of room as we sit up straight. Keep your back straight; you can fold your hands in your lap or rest one wrist on the table while eating or at rest.

This is what you can expect at Cotillion, formal receptions, banquets and balls. You will have had a formal invitation. You will be wearing formal clothing: a dinner jacket, and black or white tie (also known as a tux) or a formal ball gown (full length) with a shawl, or fur wrap and jewels. Hair will be clean and done-up off the shoulders, teeth and nails clean and tidy. Men may be wearing white gloves, which will be removed until dancing begins.

Overcoats and wraps will all be checked at the door. (If you are invited to dine in someone's home, bring a Hostess Gift and present it when you are greeted at the door.) Tables are often adjacent to the dance floor in a ballroom. There may be an orchestra, or perhaps just a piano or a harp. First there will be dinner music, and then dance music. After the meal, the party will move to the dance floor.

As soon as everyone is seated, waiters will appear and serve you. They may even put your napkin across your lap for you. They might pour water in your goblet (the biggest glass in your place setting) and offer you a dinner roll, which would be placed on your bread plate, along with a pad or ball of butter. It is appropriate to quietly say, "Thank You" when a waiter gives you something. When you ask for something while dining, always say "May I…" For example, *"May I have lemon in my water?"* When drinking, look into your glass, not over it.

Now we will set our places and practice breaking, buttering, and eating bite-sized pieces of bread. First we will all recite the rhyme and draw the place setting as we learned it in lesson one.

Place Setting Rhyme

Hey Diddle Diddle,
My plate in the Middle,
And we'll be eating soon.

My fork on the Left,
Below the bread plate,
Across from my cup and spoon.

My knife on the Right,
Its blade facing in,
And now we can begin.

TKGR

Bread and rolls are eaten in bite-sized pieces, taken one at a time. Hold the bread in one hand and break off a piece. Apply a small amount of butter with your spreader and put it in your mouth. Now we will set our places and practice breaking, buttering and eating bite-sized pieces of bread.

Often there will be a small knife lying across the bread plate for use in spreading butter. Appetizers are always served before the meal and may arrive on their own small plate and sit on top of your service plate or "charger" (the big plate sometimes found under your dinner plate). Sometimes they are on small platters which people pass around the table. Appetizers may be followed by a salad or a bowl of soup. Your waiter will provide you with any additional utensils needed, and he will remove those that have been used or will not be needed.

When you are having salad, he or she will ask if you would like pepper ground fresh onto your salad with a huge hand-held pepper grinder. Salad is eaten with your salad fork, which is the smaller fork found to the left of your dinner fork. You may cut the larger pieces of salad with your fork and knife and then rest your knife on the edge of your serving plate underneath. Then put your fork in your right hand and use it to eat your salad. Salad dressing may be applied in the kitchen or delivered in a small cup "on the side" or next to your salad so you can serve yourself.

Soup is eaten with a soup spoon, which is rounder and larger than a teaspoon. If your soup is served in a large shallow soup plate, leave your spoon in it when you are resting or finished. If it is served in a smaller bowl or cup, place your spoon on the serving plate underneath.

To eat soup, tip the spoon away from you and fill it by moving it toward the back of the soup plate or bowl. You won't forget the proper way to eat soup if you remember this saying, "Out to sea and back to me." Please do not blow on your soup if you fear it is too warm to eat. Stir hot soup to cool it. Leave your spoon in the bowl to conduct the heat out and wait. Use the side of your soup-spoon to cut vegetables, meat, noodles, etc., in your soup. Oyster crackers may be placed in the soup one or two at a time. Keep the rest on your bread and butter plate. When just a small amount of soup is left, tip the bowl away from you and use the spoon to get the rest. Leave your spoon in the empty bowl.

If the table is set without a bread plate and knife, put the bread and butter on the upper left side of your dinner plate. Use your dinner knife to spread the butter.

(Lesson 2—Quiz Time)

And that will end our lesson for today.

Teens at the Table Lesson Two

Quiz

Questions and Answers

Question 1. T/F) It is acceptable to move your name card to another seat.

Answer: False. You must sit where your host has placed you.

Question 2. T/F) When invited to the home, we should bring a gift for the hostess.

Answer: True. Yes, for example, flowers are a traditional hostess gift.

Question 3. T/F) Good posture has no effect on digestion.

Answer: False. Bad posture allows little room for stomach and lungs to function.

Question 4. T/F) Your bread plate is always on your left.

Answer: True. Your bread plate is on the left, above your fork.

Question 5. Briefly describe how a gentleman assists a lady with her chair.

Answer: He says, "May I help you?" then he pulls the chair out from the table. She says, "Yes, please," steps in front of the chair, bends her knees and begins to sit. He pushes the chair forward to touch the back of her legs, while she takes the sides of the chair in her hands and pulls it under her as she sits. He then lets go of the chair and she says, "Thank you."

Teens at the Table

Part I
Table Manners and
Good Social Behavior

Lesson 3: Best Guest Dinner Conversation

Hello again. Please find the seat where your place card is waiting and stand behind your chair. Today we will start by setting the table. First we will say the Place Setting Rhyme. All together now...

Place Setting Song

Hey Diddle Diddle,
My plate in the Middle,
And we'll be eating soon.

My fork on the Left,
Below the bread plate,
Across from my cup and spoon.

My knife on the Right,
Its blade facing in,
And now we can begin.

TKGR

We'll start with the quietest, most attentive group. Please step to the plate table and get what you need. This will be a test for you. I'm sure you can do it. This time we won't draw the place setting. After you set your place, you may be seated.

Today's lesson includes Dining Tips. We will learn about foods that are difficult to eat. We will also learn about the Art of Dinner Conversation. Can someone name a food you might call difficult to eat? Yes, that would include foods such as lobster and crab claws, which require special utensils, or fried chicken and fish and chips, which are considered finger-foods unless they are served with a main course that requires use of a knife and fork. Artichoke petals are plucked from the thistle and discarded after the soft end is nibbled. Cold asparagus can be held between the fingers and eaten whole, or sliced and eaten with a fork. Shrimp may be peeled and the shells discarded; shrimp cocktail is eaten with a small fork and the tails are discarded. At a formal dinner, watch your hostess for cues.

One dish that everyone has tried and some have difficulty with is *spaghetti,* so today we will have spaghetti noodles. We will be serving from your right side, so please lean a bit to the left when the food comes to your plate.

Keep your good posture throughout the meal. The elbow rhymes will help you to remember. Repeat after me:

"Mabel, Mabel, if you're able, Keep your elbows off the table."

The same reminder in another version:

"__Name__, __Name__, strong and able, keep your elbows off the table."

Say that to yourself often. Out of respect, say it only in private to someone else. Please wait for everyone to be served. Once everyone is served, I will show you the proper way to eat long pasta noodles, called "spaghetti." Always wait until everyone is served before you begin a meal. This is part of good table manners. Here are some other tips on dining.

Once your host or hostess has welcomed you and everyone has had a chance to meet and then be seated, someone will probably call for your attention. (This is often done by lightly tapping the edge of a goblet with the tip of a knife.) Everyone should stop what they are doing and sit at attention. Someone will probably thank you all for coming and give thanks for the meal. This is often called "Grace," and Invocation," or the "Blessing." It can be short and sweet or quite lengthy. In any case, you must sit quietly with hands folded in reverence for the duration of the words offered. Show respect for your host and hostess whenever they speak. Before you eat, wait until the hostess has put her napkin on her lap and taken the first bite.

If someone asks you to pass the salt, give him or her the salt and the pepper. They always stay together as a set. If there is no salt on the table, that probably means the meal has been salted. It would be impolite to ask for more salt. Taste every dish; you may discover a new favorite food. Don't take more food than you can finish, then wait to be excused when the host and hostess stand to leave. Always thank the hostess for inviting you and compliment her on the meal or the part you enjoyed most.

Now, let's get on with our specific lesson and dish of the day. You'll receive breadsticks on your bread plate. These don't require butter. They can be used to soak up sauce, or as a pusher. To stay neat, we aren't having sauce with the noodles. However, you may have grated cheese if you like.

Here is the proper way to eat long pasta noodles: roll a few strands at a time onto the tip of your fork. Some hosts and hostesses provide a large spoon to help you. You'll find it placed above the dinner plate. Hold it in the left hand with the fork in the right hand, or you may use the side of your plate to help roll the noodles. Shorter strands can be gathered with the tip of the fork and eaten. Please do not slurp noodles into your mouth, whipping sauce in every direction. Bite off trailing ends and return them to your plate with the fork. This takes practice, but it can be done. (We don't cut the noodles up unless we are at home eating casually, or feeding a baby.)

Another dining tip: Sometimes pasta sauce contains bay leaves, seeds or sausage. If you find something like this that doesn't feel right in your mouth, here's how to remove it. First, try to eat any of it that you can and then remove it with your spoon and place it on the edge of your plate. If it happens to be an unsightly piece of gristle or bone, silently spit it into the corner of your napkin. Then keep it folded in the napkin on your lap until you go or request a new napkin.

A big part of your responsibility as a guest is to share conversations with the other guests at your table. Customarily, conversation moves around the table to the right. However, you should also occasionally speak to the person on your left and to the person across from you. Try to include people in the conversation by asking questions such as, "What did you think of that?" or "How did you feel about that?" This will allow you to listen to them speak about themselves. People like to talk about themselves and someone who will listen is considered charming. Take care not to dominate the conversation or one person's attention. Take turns listening.

It is easier to eat while listening than while you are speaking, and you must never speak with food in your mouth. If you notice that someone hasn't been able to stop talking long enough to eat, say something to carry the conversation for a minute or change the subject and give the person a break. Everyone should dine at about the same pace so that various courses of the meal can be prepared and put on the table together. It is a team effort between the diners, the servers, and the kitchen to have everything stay on schedule.

Never say or do anything *offensive* at the table. This includes vulgar language, rude or animalistic behavior, descriptions of wounds, illnesses, surgeries or accidents, etc. These subjects tend to put people off and make them lose their appetites. This would be an insult to your host and hostess, because they want everyone to enjoy the meal they have so thoughtfully provided.

Other conversation taboos include politics and religion. These are very personal subjects about which people tend to become emotional—even passionate. At a formal dining affair, people are expected to control emotions and behave as ladies and gentlemen. Your dining table should stay on a fairly even keel—steady as she goes as a big ship at sea. Don't "rock the boat." Controversial subjects will not be welcome and should be left at the door. Part of the reality of Etiquette Lessons is that we have 0-tolerance for bad language and disruptive behavior. Offenders will be dismissed.

Let's talk about Personality. Consider these sayings:

"If you can't say anything nice, don't say anything at all." "Even a cat can look at the queen!" Each of these expressions, in its own way, refers to the obvious fact that no one can read your mind. You can think, have strong opinions and believe what you will, but in good company you must be polite, agreeable and get along. America is a free country and everyone has certain rights; remember "Life, Liberty and the Pursuit of Happiness." We can't all be best friends, but we need to be tolerant of each other. We must agree that others have a right to be different from us. One episode of bad behavior should be considered a mistake which can be corrected.

Sometimes we meet people with abrasive personalities, even at a formal affair. "Abrasive" in this case means some one who is prone to being overly critical, defensive, negative or complaining. Less annoying but equally anti-social people include people who tend to have arrogant, overly passive, noncommittal, or insulting personalities. The best policy is to recognize these traits and avoid being their target. Use your best manners and be polite, no matter what. Treat everyone with the same courtesy. If they are smart, they will come along. Creating or participating in a "scene" could have one removed from the guest list. If someone annoys you, let it go. Imitate the man who said, "I never met a fellow I didn't like!" As much as possible, be on good terms with everyone. Keep in mind that you are fulfilling the roles of Ladies and Gentlemen. Others will soon learn that you are predictably well-mannered and able to act with civility and social grace.

Say we are at a dinner party and Snow White is our hostess. Who do we have sitting at the table with us? Give me several names, please. Who would you be? Of course we would have to include Grumpy, Bashful, Sleepy, Happy, and who else? Now that we have our tablemates, with a variety of personalities, let's have a conversation. This ball will represent our conversation, and we will toss it around when we address each other. When attending a dinner party, you must come prepared. Remember to bring at least one joke, a compliment, an article of news, check the weather and know current events like the score of the latest "big game" if there is one.

We'll start with Miss or Mr. Happy. What do you do first when you want to speak to someone? How do you properly address someone at the dinner table? Yes, you call them by their name, and what else? You call them by their name and *title*, yes. Then, and only then, do you have their attention and the attention of others who will want to hear his answer. Now you can toss them the ball and ask a question. They in turn will toss the ball back and answer, or hold the ball while answering you, then call someone else's name and toss the ball to them with a new question. For example, "Miss or Mr. Happy (toss the ball), how did you meet our hostess, Miss Snow White?"

"I met her at a garden party last summer."

"Mr. Grumpy (toss), how did you meet Miss Snow White?" We'll take turns until every one has shared in the conversation. You see, no matter what their personalities are like, each dinner guest is expected to engage in conversation.

Try not to "drop the ball" by not answering a question. Remember, we are indoors and using the ball as a symbol for conversation. Please pay attention to what we are doing; be quiet and keep the conversation going.

Once in a blue moon (not very often) you may be given a fingerbowl before dessert. It will be placed in front of you, as a small bowl with a doily under it on a desert plate, with a dessert fork on the plate beside the bowl on the left, and a teaspoon on the plate to the right of the bowl. Using both hands, pick up the finger bowl and doily and place them on the table to the upper left of your dessert plate for later use. Place the utensils on the table. Dessert will be served on your plate. Eat your dessert with your spoon in the right hand, using the fork in your left hand as a pusher. When finished, place the fork and spoon on the plate for removal. Lastly, pick up the finger bowl and doily and place them in front of you. Dip fingertips of each hand in turn into the bowl and dry them with your napkin. Place the napkin in loose folds on the left as you leave the table.

(Lesson 3—Quiz Time)

That ends the lesson for today.

Teens at the Table, Part I Lesson 3
Quiz
Questions and Answers

Question 1. T/F) We should cut spaghetti noodles into small pieces.

Answer: True, but only when we feed them to babies.

Question 2. T/F) Salt and pepper are passed together as a set.

Answer: True, even if someone just asks for salt.

Question 3. How does one start a conversation?

Answer: Begin with the person's title and say their name to get their attention.

Question 4. Before making an announcement or a toast, what is the proper way to get everyone's attention?

Answer: Very lightly tap the top edge of your goblet with the tip of the back of your dinner knife.

Question 5. What subjects are not appropriate for dinner conversation?

Answer: Never say or do anything offensive during dinner. This includes vulgar language, rude or animalistic behavior, descriptions of wounds, illnesses, surgeries or accidents, etc. Other conversation taboos include politics and religion.

Teens at the Table

Part I
Table Manners and
Good Social Behavior

Lesson 4: Host with the Most
Dinner Conversation

Hello, everyone. We will begin with a bit of protocol instruction. Who can define the word *protocol* as in *computer protocol?* The term, "computer protocol" is a set of rules that govern the format of messages exchanged between computers.

Likewise, in the human world, *protocol* is all the customs and regulations of diplomatic formality and etiquette. Diplomatic formalities are the basic rules of meeting others in a social setting. In this lesson we will deal with some of the protocol and basic good manners of *Introductions.* I am talking about the handshake, bow, and curtsey. As soon as everyone has washed their hands or used hand sanitizer, we will begin. Please form a line or two here, facing me.

Say you have just given a performance or received an award at a school assembly. Everyone is applauding. It is appropriate for you to hesitate, then take a bow or curtsey to acknowledge and thank the audience before leaving the stage. It will also signal the audience that they can stop applauding.

Etiquette Lessons

Girls, this is how to curtsey: lightly lift both sides of your skirt, or if you are wearing slacks, raise your arms out to the sides to keep your balance. In one smooth motion, shift your weight to the left leg, bend your knees, tap your right toe behind you, lower your eyes and nod your head. The deeper the curtsey, the more reverence and appreciation is conveyed. Sometimes, you may even want to place your hand over your heart during a curtsey. When being introduced on stage you may curtsey, but keep your chin up. Maintain eye contact so the audience can see your face. All the young ladies, please try a curtsey together. Thank you. That looks very nice.

Now for the gentlemen; a bow is taken, bending from the waist with knees straight and a nod of the head, either with your hands at your sides or more formally, with your hands behind you or with your right hand over your heart and your left hand behind you. Gentlemen, altogether, take a bow. Thank you. Please note: we live in a society where direct eye contact is expected and welcomed as a form of communication. Everyone should remember to use eye contact often.

When you are introducing two people to each other, name the person of higher rank or age first. For example, "Grandmother, this is my teacher, Mr. Hendriks." Or, "Mr. Hendriks, this is my friend, Jennifer." Remember to use a title when introducing adults: Mr., Mrs., Ms., Dr., etc. This is a way of showing respect. Ask people if they have a personal preference in how you address them on a regular basis. (Being on a "first name" basis should be considered a privilege.)

When you are introducing someone to a group, make a gesture toward that person, telling a little something about them to queue the conversation. For example, "I would like you all to meet my cousin Nick, who just flew in from Boston; he plays the trumpet."

Air kisses and other greetings such as the slight bow or curtsey or even a gentle kiss on the top of the hand may occur, but normally a *handshake* is expected when you meet both ladies and gentlemen, especially in business.

A gentleman will tip his hat to greet a lady, and he will always remove his hat indoors.

This is how a proper handshake is done: with your right hand, firmly grasp the other person's right hand, palm to palm. Together, pump your hands once and release. Again, your hands will come together, rise up, go down and come up again with the release. Let's try it.

Walk past me on the way to find your seats, stopping to give me your handshake.

Please find your seat and stand behind it. Before you are seated, gentlemen, remember to offer to help the ladies with their chairs.

Next, you will each pretend that you are planning to have a party. Let's say it is your Birthday Party. We must write the invitations, and since we should expect to receive a few gifts, we shall also practice composing thank you notes. We won't need place settings today, because we will be having finger-food appetizers, and they will be served after we do some writing. You'll find an index card and a pen on your placemat.

You will receive your beverage now. Hold the cup for the pourer, please. In a formal dining room, your waiter will usually pick up your goblet, fill it and return it to the upper right of your place setting. He will also remove any wine glasses you will obviously not need. Beverages are served from the right, so lean a little to the left to be out of the way.

Until now, we have been learning general good manners and the etiquette of being a good dinner guest. When you give a party, *you* are the host or hostess, and that means you have certain responsibilities to your guests. First of all, you need to send them an invitation. We must make sure they know the "four W's" of our event. Who can guess what I mean when I refer to the four W's?

Raise your hand if you can tell me the first of the four W's. The first is "Who." Who is the birthday party for? You, of course, so write the word, "Who" (with a colon after it), and then write your name.

Now we need the other three W's. Who can tell me the second W? That's right; it's "What," meaning what kind of party? Now write "What:" and then add "Birthday Party" on the same line.

Now our guests will know we are having a birthday party. What else do they need to know? What are the third and fourth W's?

Who knows the third? You may have learned this in journalism. Newspaper articles have the four W's. Yes, "When" is next. We must inform our guests when the party will be. That includes the date and the time. On the third line write "When:" and then write your date and time. For example, Saturday, November 8, 2:30–5:30 PM.

Who knows what to write on the last line? Yes, "Where:". Our guests need to know where the party will be held. On the fourth line of your invitation, write "Where:" and the location of your party.

Written in this order on your invitation,

<u>The "Four W's" of Invitations are:</u>
WHO: whose party is it?
WHAT: what is the occasion?
WHEN: when is the party?
WHERE: where is the party?

Can you think of anything else that should go on the invitation? The guests need more information. A proper invitation has additional information in the lower left and the lower right corners.

I'll give you a hint; it has to do with your guest's responsibilities. Yes, they must know how to let you know if they plan to attend your party. They must give you a response. How can they do this? Invitation protocol requires that you provide them with—what? Yes, RSVP. They need a phone number and the name of someone who is waiting to hear their response. In the lower left corner of the invitation write the letters RSVP, followed by a phone number. You should also give them the date by which you need to know how many guests are coming and the name of someone who is waiting for their call. Who knows the meaning of the term "RSVP"? Of course, it means, "Respond, if you please," or in the original French, *"Repondez vous s'il vous plait."*

Now you will be served appetizers. Please eat quietly while the lesson continues. A word about the food: here we have some brie (which is a very soft cheese), paté (paste made from meat), caviar (fish roe or eggs, usually sturgeon) and sour cream on crackers with a variety of olives. These are just a few of many types of appetizers. Please try a taste of everything. I think you will like it.

The discussion of RSVP gives us an opportunity to practice telephone etiquette. I have two telephones to practice with. We'll take turns confirming that we will or will not attend someone's party. When I make the sound of a phone ringing, you will answer, using proper telephone etiquette and say, for example:

"Hello, Mc Williams residence, Elsie speaking."

Then the other student will tell you the reason for the call, saying first, *"Hello, this is Grant calling, may I speak to Charles?"*

(Ask your parents for family rules on telephone safety. What do they want you to tell people who call for them when they are not at home? I suggest you say, "They are busy, may I have them call you back?" When in doubt, take simple messages of name and telephone number; details can be very confusing.)

A very formal affair like a wedding will often require an invitation with a response card included, along with stamped envelope for return post. Guests can simply mark the card and send it back, stating their intentions. This saves guests from long distance phone calls and allows a third person, like a wedding planner for example, to manage the guest list. Some invitations include maps to an event. If guests are traveling some distance, the formal invitation might include nearby hotel and restaurant information as well.

What information about our party should we provide in the lower right corner of our invitation? What else does your guest need to know? Does the party have a theme? Is it, for example, a swimming party? If so, your guests should be prepared to bring their swim wear. That's right, it is the host or hostess's responsibility to advise quests of what to wear to his or her party. You want your guests to dress appropriately so that they will feel at ease and not be over-dressed or under-dressed. Attire notes go in the lower right corner on your invitation.

I'll come around and check your work. Your birthday party invitation should have the four W's, the RSVP, and attire notes.

You may also include a map. Send the invitations out at least two weeks ahead of the party, allowing time for people to fit your event into their schedule. Ask for the Responses or RSVP's to come back three days ahead to allow time for food preparation. Wedding invitations can go out as early as three months ahead to allow people to arrange for time off from work and make travel arrangements.

Now, let's say the party was a big success and our guests have given us something for our birthday. What do you think they might have given us? That's right, gifts. Please turn your invitations over because now we will write a Thank You Note on the back of the index card. A *Thank You Note* should be short and personal. For example:

Dear Donald,
Name the gift and what you like about it. Thank them for coming to your Party. End the note in a polite way, signing with something like
Your friend,
Harold

Thank You Notes are not just for gifts. Guests who had a great time may want to show their appreciation by sending a short note like this, for example:

"Dear Jill,
Thank you for inviting me to your wonderful home for the garden party. You are the perfect hostess!
Your friend,
Gail"

Just for fun, write a thank you note to the person across from you, pretending that they have given you a birthday gift. We will take turns reading the thank you notes.

Remember, you want your Thank You Note to bring a smile to the face of the person who receives it when they read it, just as they brought a smile to yours.

(Lesson 4—Quiz Time)

Teens at the Table, Part I Lesson 4

Quiz

Questions and Answers

Question 1.) What are the 4 W's of a proper Invitation?
Answer: Who What When and Where

Question 2.) Define the word "Protocol."
Answer: Protocol is a set of rules that govern meetings.

Question 3.) When introducing a lady & gentleman, whose name do you say first?
Answer: Say the lady's name first, as "Ms. Jennifer, I'd like you to meet Mr. Robert." You are presenting him to her.

Question 4.) Which hand do we always shake hands with?
Answer: We always shake hands with the right hand while giving eye contact..

Question 5.) What are the 5 points of a proper Thank You Note?
Answer: 1.) Write the person's name, of course.

2.) Name the actual gift.

3.) Tell something you like about it.

4.) Thank them for attending your event.

5.) Write a friendly closing and sign it with your first name.

Teens at the Table

Part II
American Cotillion

Teens at the Table

Part II
American Cotillion

Lesson 5: Fine Dining Vocabulary, Types of Service, Menus, Terms, History of Fine Dining in the American Culture

Welcome back. Find your place at the table. Gentlemen, please assist the ladies with their chairs and we will begin. Today we will study fine dining vocabulary. We will also practice eating soup and salad.

Formal dining rooms employ many staff members who wear white gloves. They may parade platters of decorated food around the room before serving. This can add fun and excitement to dining, especially if you are having Cherries Jubilee or Baked Alaska (the flaming deserts).

Banquet food is served in one of the following ways:

Plate Service (often called <u>American Service</u>). Whether or not the food intended for the meal has been displayed first, each individual plate of food is made up in the kitchen and then brought to the table.

<u>Sideboard Service</u> (Food is displayed on a high, narrow table, standing by the dining room wall near the dining table.) Each

plate is filled by the waiter or Butler/Maid, at the sideboard and then served to the guest.

English Service (Food platters are displayed on a table or cart.) Seated guests serve themselves from serving platters held by waiters.

When guests are asked to serve themselves from the side table, the service is known as "buffet."

Family-style Service. (Various foods intended for the meal are placed on the table in serving dishes.) Each individual will serve himself and then pass it on. In this case, we pass the serving platters to our right. Remember, service always comes in from the left and moves on and out to the right.

French Service, *traditionally used in the White House.* (This style of service is considered the epitome of elegance and is the one in which in which the service staff serves each guest individually from silver platters.)

Dishes may be carried from guest to guest and served by one wait-person or prepared and rolled along on a cart while being served by another. Your plate may be picked up and filled from dishes on a side table with selections you have made. You will be asked questions about how you would like your food served. Who can tell me what some of those questions might be? Yes, you would first be asked to choose a beverage. Water with lemon or ginger ale are good choices for young people. A good waiter will tell you what is on the menu, describing each dish and what goes with it. They should be willing and helpful in making suggestions if you are not sure what you want. Dining rooms usually have men dressed in black and white to take orders and do the serving.

Just a note on paying for the meal: If you invite someone to dine, you must pay the bill, and if you are the guest, graciously say, "Thank you" and then reciprocate when you can. A tip, or gratuity, is probably included in the bill; if not, add 15–20% for the waiter, depending upon how good the service was.

Often you will have many dishes to choose from and many decisions to make. Your palate, or appreciation of the tastes of different foods will grow with your knowledge and experience.

Some menus simply tell us what to expect, as on a set menu chosen for a banquet.

The Seven-Course Meal
Will start with 1st a Soup Course,
2nd a Fish Course,
3rd a Sorbet Course,
4th a Meat or Poultry Course,
5th a Salad Course,
6th the Dessert Course
and finally, 7th the Coffee Course.

Once guests are settled in their chairs, the host and hostess will call for everyone's attention. Wine is served with the first course. Everyone waits for the hostess to put her napkin on her lap and for the host to raise his glass for a toast, welcoming the guests to this auspicious occasion. Then they may pause to say a blessing or give thanks for the meal. After the blessing and the welcoming toast, everyone takes a sip from their beverage and the meal begins.

Dining etiquette and good social behavior belong at home too. For example, here is a bit of everyday etiquette: If friends visit your home, invite them in, introduce them to your family, offer them a seat and a beverage. (Most people appreciate a glass of ice water.) This is the traditional routine for making people feel welcome, whether we are in a formal dining room or not.

A second toast may be made as the 6th course, the Dessert Course, is served. This time the toast will be to the Guest of Honor, the Chef, or to indicate a special announcement. With the 7th Course, the Coffee Course, music and dancing begin.

Banquets are easy; you are simply served and haven't many decisions to make. Ordering from a menu is another thing entirely and can be daunting until you learn what you like. Fine restaurant and club menus used in formal dining rooms all over America display a vast selection of foods and beverages from which to choose. We will familiarize you with a typical menu. Let's look at some menus or imagine them and describe what we can expect to see.

At a typical dinner, beverage orders will be taken first and then you will be asked to select an appetizer, soup or salad, an entrée or main course with a choice of vegetables and starch, then dessert, and beverage to go with the dessert. Some of these are served together, making it a three or four-course meal lasting one or two hours. Lunch and breakfast are much quicker.

The American traditions in fine dining began in Northern Europe. As our culture has matured, it has diversified, adding new foods with old favorites to serve the sophisticated palate or sense of taste. A modern host, hostess and chef may select from many choices to serve in the seven courses in a formal banquet. You will learn to expect creativity and variety in fine dining and the world of gourmet chefs. It is a good idea to sample and learn the names of as many types of foods as you can so you can recognize different foods when they are presented to you. You probably have some favorites already. Who has a favorite dish?

Continental fare includes food from at least 2 continents—European and American. A sophisticated menu may also offer dishes prepared with influences from Asia, Mexico, Greece, Polynesia or other places. Some special dishes are eaten only at ethnic or religious gatherings. Part of the fun in fine dining is discovering and learning how to eat new foods. You can be sure, though, that your basic dining etiquette will remain the same while you sample all the possibilities. The roots of our fine dining vocabulary are derived from France, Italy and England.

Familiar Terms from the French Menu: *Du jour* means "Of the day"; a *soup du jour* entree is the first or main item ordered. **Au jus** is a light sauce of meat juice. Hollandaise is a lemon and butter sauce. Sauteé means to fry lightly. Croutons are dried bread squares. Poulet is chicken. Poisson is fish. Bernaise is a white sauce with herbs for meat.

Italian dining includes many types of pasta, or noodles. *Al dente* means, firmly cooked pasta. Who knows some other Italian terms?

It is time to set the table and dine. Today, when you make your place setting, place the bowl in the center of your dinner plate or service plate. Repeat the Place Setting Rhyme together.

Place Setting Rhyme

Hey Diddle Diddle

My plate in the Middle,

And we'll be eating soon.

My fork on the Left,
Below the bread plate,
Across from my cup and spoon.

My knife on the Right,
Its blade facing in,
And now we can begin.

TKGR

History of Culture in America

During the sixteenth century, refined Italian table manners known as "etiquette" became popular with royalty in France and England. The word "etiquette" is derived from the name of a special card or ticket allowing entrance to royal court events. Only the privileged, trained in fine table manners and social behavior, were invited to dine. A will to conform still proceeds opportunity for advancement among civilized people. People relax when those around them behave in a predictable manner. When a group's rules of protocol and etiquette are observed, each member is allowed in turn the opportunity to attract or charm and entertain others. This protocol remains, no matter who the leaders of a particular group may be. Most members simply advance. A few alter tradition. Some make sweeping changes.

Seventeenth century revolutions turned the tables in France and England. Everything became the property of the people, including etiquette and political protocol. Liberty from ruling monarchs brought every man freedom and sovereignty. In

America this began with the Continental Congress, the Declaration of Independence, the Constitution of the United States, and the Bill of Rights. In America, virtually every man is king in his own castle. Every woman is queen in hers. In the eyes of loving adults, all girls are Princesses and boys are Prince Charming.

Early Americans practiced European traditions of fine dining and social grace. New styles were imported with newcomers or added out of necessity. Pioneers moved westward, setting tables across the nation with heirloom linens, tableware and prayer books they had packed in trunks. Ladies and gentlemen in government, military, education, religion and all professions socialized at countless gatherings, both casual and formal, to establish a strong foundation for our great country.

Nineteenth century American culture emanated from centers of industry and government. From New England came propriety, decorum, and the arts, confidence from the sheer power and magnetism of New York and legendary spirit and hospitality of the South. We developed a successful two-party system of government, electing dynamic leaders with term limitations. Moving West, we added bold business in oil and cattle, automobiles, the gold rush in California, railroads, electricity, telephones and National Parks.

The twentieth century brought more immigration, Hollywood with powerful imagery of glamorous lifestyles, sports to entertain us, airplanes for transport, freeway systems, war in the Pacific and Europe, the annexation of Hawaii and Alaska, income tax and Social Security, television with more lifestyle imagery, space travel, plastics, communication satellites, computers, newcomers from Asia, Mexico and the Near East, higher education for the masses, longer life-span through modern medicine, increased foreign trade and foreign affairs, the internet, and Homeland Defense.

In the twenty-first century, America is confident, compassionate and creative. We are the world's partner in the existence of democracy. Over seven generations have brought the USA's culture to this point. Ethnic strands from around the world are woven daily into American's tablecloth. The central point in the American home is a dining table with a good deal of tradition behind it. Our concerns are global, yet some things never change. Casual and formal dining and socializing in the Western tradition still sustains the growth of our culture.

Family, friends and loved ones sit at our table with us to dine. We prepare meals and make celebrations for each other here. We share important discussions and announcements here. Our holidays are here, even as picnics set outside or formal banquets in ballrooms. This is where we give thanks and honor our ancestors.

Once known as "charm school," etiquette and manners training has flourished periodically as a pillar of civilized culture. This is especially important as we add many new members to our society from other cultures and because of rapid changes in lifestyle. Due to the pursuit of higher education or demanding work schedules, many families have not practiced traditional fine dining at home. Perhaps etiquette training at home skipped a generation or two because of distances between family members or information about traditions was sketchy or incomplete. Many modern meals are fast food or pizza, eaten with the hands in front of the TV or in the family car between school, sports, and other after-school activities.

The word "charm" means a power of pleasing or attracting. It is a continuous power, exerted with the practice of good etiquette and peaceful exchange. The human race thrives on social interaction. We form interest groups and families to make places for everyone. We don't have to become best friends with everyone. Allowing room and respect for each other and for diverse traditions gains us peace. Charm is the magnetism which allows us to dwell peacefully within a community and make progress.

Each generation of Americans embraces and refines the Western fine dining tradition. Now it is your turn. You are the ladies and gentlemen of the future. You will soon be interviewed, invited, and presented at all sorts of social events. You will one day be a guest of honor, host, or join other guests at receptions, attend cotillions, toast the bride and groom, dine with VIPs, and have lunch with the boss. Now you know the history. Civilized people participate together in fine dining and formal social situations for the evolution of society. It is perfectly natural for you to step forward and take your place as a civilized member of society.

Now that everyone has been served, we may continue. The soup course is the first course in a seven-course banquet. It is now that the host will begin the meal by offering a toast to welcome everyone. Later on, perhaps at the beginning of the dessert course, he will offer a toast to the guest of honor.

Chilled soup may be served in a specialized, ice-lined bowl on a stem, but the technique for eating soup is the same, no matter what type of bowl it is in. Today we will practice with a standard soup bowl, using a standard round soupspoon. The proper technique for lifting the soup from the bowl to the mouth is to hold the spoon parallel to the table between your thumb and pointer finger, with your thumb on top. Push the spoon just below the surface of the soup *away from you* to fill it, then bring the liquid to your lips and sip quietly while pouring it into your mouth. To recall the proper way to fill your spoon again, it might help to remember this old saying:

"Out to sea and back to me."

Between sips, when the soup course is finished, leave the soupspoon in the bowl or on the dish beneath the bowl.

Our second dish today will be like a fifth course, known as the Salad Course. It may be eaten with the knife and fork or with just the fork held in the right hand. If cheese is served with the salad, it can be placed with your bread, butter and bread knife on the bread plate and eaten from there like meat or fish with the knife and fork. Grissini bread sticks, or other types of crackers or bread may be used as pushers to nudge that last bit of lettuce onto your fork. When you have finished the salad course, place your knife and fork in the finished position across the salad plate.

(Lesson 5—Quiz Time)

That ends the lesson for today. Thank you.

Teens at the Table, Part II, Cotillion, Lesson 5
Quiz
Questions and Answers

Question 1. There are <u>5</u> types of Banquet Food Service: Plate Service, Sideboard Service, English Service, French Service, Family Style and Buffet. What is the most common type of Food Service used in formal dining rooms in America today?

Answer: Plate Service (often called <u>American Service</u>.) Each plate of food is prepared in the kitchen and brought to the table.

Question 2. Name the three documents that guarantee America's Freedom?

Answer: The Declaration of Independence, The United States Constitution, and The Bill of Rights.

Question 3. T/F Everyone lifts a glass when a toast is made.

Answer: **False.** If someone proposes a toast to you, do not raise your glass. Smile, say "Thank you," and be prepared to give a quick speech.

Question 4. Name the courses of a seven-course banquet.

Answer: 1st, Soup; 2nd, Fish; 3rd, Sorbet; 4th, Meat or Poultry; 5th Salad; 6th, Dessert; and 7th, Coffee Course.

Question 5.   Write or recite the rhyme that describes the proper way to fill your soupspoon before sipping.

Answer: "Out to sea and back to me."

Teens at the Table

Part II
American Cotillion

Lesson 6: Dinner Conversation Topics, Slang, Telephone Game, Punch Service, Personalities, American Slow Dance

Welcome back; find your place at the table and we will begin. Today we start with dinner conversation. "No man is an island." What is the meaning of this phrase? Yes, it means that we all need other people to function, to feel complete, and to share progress in our lives. We all advance together—in our schools, in our community, and as a nation, etc. We need social interaction. We need society.

Once perceived as an opportunity rather than a challenge, one learns to navigate the seas of dining conversation with many fascinating companions. It is through communication that we get what we want and how we evaluate the needs of others.

The goal of society is advancement for each person, advancement for society as a whole, and even for the entire human race. Advancement is gained through the exchange of thoughts and ideas, usually shared over a meal. Each individual at a table brings something to the mix of conversation and contributions are shared by all.

Let's observe this with a demonstration of verbal exchange. This is a game called "Telephone." We start a comment at this end of the room. Whisper the comment to the person next to you on your right until it works its way back here. We will serve refreshments and continue the lecture while you quietly share the comment to the person on your right after you hear it from the person on your left. We'll start with you. The secret comment, ("A bear came into the room with a frog on his head.") is written on this paper. Keep the paper and pass the idea along.

Today we need only dessert plates, napkins, cups, and spoons. You'll be having a snack similar to the Sorbet Course in a seven-course meal, with light crackers. After the snack and a bit more lecture, we'll begin our lesson on American slow dance and the waltz.

Who will help serve today? We need two volunteers to assist with serving punch. We need one to pour and one to serve. Thank you.

After you have been seated at a formal affair, the next challenge is *What will you say?* What do you bring to the conversation? We know we should prepare for a social event by reading or listening to the news or watching it on TV so we are up on current events. We should also keep a repertoire of opening comments, jokes and compliments to help carry lulls in conversation.

Think of something interesting and not too controversial to bring up. Know yourself. What can you talk about at length without being a bore, making things up or exaggerating?

Ask questions. Make a quick evaluation of your table partners. Is there someone there whom you want to get to know? Is there someone who has information that would be helpful to you? If you are with a group of new acquaintances and one or two people you know, you may want to ask for an introduction. You'll find it important to compose intelligent questions to get someone talking so that you can listen and learn more about them. Of course if there is someone in the party you would like to dance with later, secure an introduction now so that she will be more comfortable when you approach her, and you can say her name when you ask her to dance.

Who has a good joke to share today? Here's one: Why didn't Cinderella play soccer? Because she always ran away from the ball!

By the way, it is time to see how that secret message is doing. Has it come all the way around the table? Please write it down and we'll compare it now with the original. We will learn if the message changed in meaning as it went from person to person. How has it changed? What can we learn from this? Yes, you can't always believe what you hear. Don't participate in gossip and hearsay. Something that starts out innocent can end up causing trouble. Always give people the benefit of the doubt and remember, in America people are innocent until proven guilty.

As you know, there are several different types of personalities you are likely to come across at formal affairs. Some take themselves very seriously and seem not to have any fun, while others go overboard trying to be the life of the party. Be relaxed and composed, with your attention shared between other guests and your host's program. Strive to elevate the conversation. Let your presence be uplifting, quiet, and encouraging to others.

Now, since we are going to concentrate on dancing soon, we will have our quiz on lesson 6 at this time.

(Lesson 6—Quiz Time)

Be mindful of events around you and at other tables. Think ahead, watch the time, and anticipate changes in the room. For example, be prepared when the music begins by taking time in advance to practice a few ballroom and contemporary dance steps. Next we will have an introduction to the basic American slow dance. Everyone up and line up—young ladies in one line facing young gentlemen, please. Move to the gentlemen's side of the room Now ladies, starting with your right foot, walk slowly backward four steps toward the middle of the room. (1) & (2) & (3) & (4) &.

Ok, now go back toward the gentlemen. Now, pair off. I want you to walk together, ladies walking backward starting with their right foot and gentlemen walking forward starting on their left foot. You can swing your arms, but don't touch yet. (1) & (2) & (3) & (4) &. Good. Now go back. (1) & (2) & (3) & (4) &. At our next lesson we will try this to music.

The American Slow Dance
Dance to "Born Free" Composed by John Barry

This is our easy-going, beginning ballroom dance. It is ideal for getting started slowly on the dance floor as everyone settles into the rhythm of the music. First, the couple establishes a classic closed-dancing position by standing normally with feet slightly apart, facing each other. The lady's right foot is in between the man's feet. The gentleman's right hand is under the lady's left arm and below her shoulder blade, while her left arm is lying on his right arm. Her left hand is on his right shoulder, elbows lifted slightly to allow for easy movement. On the other side, their hands are in the palm-to-palm grip, lifted to the lady's shoulder height so that the couple comfortably maintains an upright posture. The gentleman always takes the lead and establishes a direction for the couple by gently guiding the lady with the tips of his right hand fingers on her back and stepping out on his left foot first. He simply takes two steps out and two steps back and she follows in corresponding movements, shifting their weight as they go. This is like walking to the beat of the music.

The Basic Step of the American slow dance goes like this:

Simultaneously, the gentleman steps toward the lady with his left foot (1) as she steps back on her right. That movement shifts his weight to his left foot (&) and her weight to her right foot in the first two beats of the music.

On the count of (2), he then takes a step toward her on his right foot, shifting his weight to his right foot as it lands on (&); meanwhile, she lifts her left foot and moves it back a step, shifting her weight back to her left foot as she puts it down. Repeat those steps and then reverse the direction as the lady steps toward the gentleman for 4 counts. Think as you go: (1 = lift) (and = down) (2 = lift) (and = down) (3 = lift) (and = down) (4 = lift) (and = down). Then repeat in the opposite direction up to the count of (8 = lift) (and = down). Do this until you begin to feel comfortable doing the basic step. We'll try it together through the entire song. After you start the dance with the Basic Step and feel comfortable on the dance floor, you may add the following:

This next step is called the "Hesitation step" because you lift one foot and put it back down in the same place and step out with the other, rocking from side to side to the (1) & (2) & beat. This gives the dance a more relaxed look, especially if you add a little bounce by bending the knees when you step out to the side. Let's try the Hesitation step. This is your chance to relax a little. When you step out you can also look that way and straighten your arm a little to emphasize the change in direction. You may eventually, later in the dance, even try a dip during the Hesitation step. Use this step for eight counts before you change directions or turn. We'll try those two steps together now.

To turn or rotate at some point, the gentleman can begin a Rotation step, slowly turning to his left and leading with his left elbow, so to speak, turning as he steps around. The lady will follow. Once confident in these basic steps, the couple can put them together into a simple routine of Forward and Hesitation-Side-to-Side, then Backward and the Rotation. The natural finish to the Rotation would of course be a spin. The gentleman may try an inward spin by lifting the lady's right hand and moving it toward her left shoulder while releasing her with his right hand to twirl around. Try a spin in slow motion. Very nice, you can also spin outward, but the inward spin is easier to control and looks very graceful in the slow dances. At our next lesson we will review these moves and go on to the Introduction to the waltz. Thank you.

Teens at the Table, Part II Cotillion, Lesson 6
Final Quiz
Questions and Answers

Question 1.) What is the meaning of the phrase, "No man is an island."

Answer: We all need other people to exist, to feel complete, and to share the progression of our lives. We all advance together. We need social interaction. We need society and we find it in our schools, our communities our places of worship, in our State, and in our Nation.

Question 2.) What is the goal of society?

Answer: The goal of society is advancement for each person, advancement for society as a whole, and even for the entire human race. Personal advancement is gained through the exchange of thoughts and ideas, usually shared over a meal.

Question 3.) What is the sixth course of a 7-Course Banquet?

Answer: Dessert, and it comes with after dinner beverages, Toasts, Announcements.

Question 4.) In Ballroom Dance, which foot does the lady always start on?

Answer: Her right.

Question 5.) In Ballroom Dance, which foot does the gentleman always start on?

Answer: His left.

Teens at the Table

Part II
American Cotillion

Lesson 7: Dressing for Dinner

(Instructor may choose to invite
Image Professionals to speak)

Welcome back; find your place at the table and we will begin. Today we are going to discuss proper attire for a formal occasion such as a Debutante Ball (a Sweet-sixteen Party for several girls) or Cotillion (Formal Dance and Banquet for young people). We will also talk a little about personal hygiene. Later, we will have light refreshments and continue Introduction to Ballroom Dance. Please note, the next lesson will be the last in this course of "Teens at the Table, Etiquette Lessons."

So, You've just received your invitation to that very special formal occasion. What do you ask yourself immediately? That's right, you ask yourself, "What should I wear?" The next thought for young ladies is usually "How should I wear my hair?"

Hair

At formal affairs a young lady's hair should be styled and done up off the shoulders. For gentlemen it should be neat, trimmed and off the collar.

Teeth

They should be clean, white and sparkling. Even if you have braces, diligent cleaning and checking the mirror often will pay off if you want others to feel comfortable being close to you.

Nails

Fingernails should be kept neatly trimmed, filed and manicured. Ladies with open-toe shoes need pedicures, too.

Shoes

A gentleman's shoes should be of lightweight leather, made for dancing. Ideally, they should be dress shoes with leather soles.

A lady's dancing shoes should have a one-inch heel or more, with an ankle strap for added support. For the desired effect of being "light on her feet," she should be able to lift herself up on the balls of her feet while dancing.

Jewelry

Less is more where jewelry is concerned for the formal affair. Now is the time to wear your birthstones, any real gemstones such as onyx and pearls, precious or semi-precious stones, and crystal tiaras. Only one ring on each hand, please.

Black Tie (Evening affairs, after six p.m.)

For the ladies, this means a chic, beaded dress or high fashion evening dress of fine fabric. A basic black dress can be acceptable with proper accessorizing. "White tie" means a long, formal gown with complimentary wrap and perhaps with matching shoes, long white gloves, tiaras, and up-dos.

For gentlemen, "*black tie*" means exactly that: black dinner jacket, dress slacks and black bow tie, with a proper white shirt, a black *cummerbund*, shirt studs and cuff links (usually gold, mother-of-pearl, or onyx), and appropriate shoes; they may be laced or slip-on, preferably of the highest quality patent leather.

For a **White Tie** affair, gentlemen wear a black-tail coat with white shirt, tie and white *waist coat* (a vest). A *cummerbund* is not acceptable to wear with a tailcoat. White gloves and top hats may be worn. Inquire in advance just how formal the event will be. At Debutante Balls and Cotillions, gentlemen and ladies may wear white gloves for dancing.

There are many types of bow ties for men to choose from for black tie events. The most common black tie for young men is the clip-on. Every young man should also have a jacket or blazer to wear with a dress shirt, slacks and tie. Young men will need to learn to tie the knot in their necktie. The most popular knot worn in America is called the Windsor knot. It was invented by the Duke of Windsor in 1936. They say that a well-tied knot is one of the first serious steps in a man's life. Of course until that time, there are clip-ons. Are there any questions about dressing for dinner?

At banquets, a sorbet, Italian Ice, or sorbet or flavored ice is served after the meat course to clear the palate. For this service all we need is our dessert plate and a spoon, water, or other beverage. This will free our time for dancing.

When the music begins, we will need six couples on the dance floor to start. May I have three young gentlemen and three young lady volunteers?

The basic Waltz step is known the *box step*, because it is like drawing a square with your feet in six beats—three beats at a time in a three count tempo: (1) (2) &(3) & (1) (2) &(3) etc. We step forward on our left and backward on our right.

We move straight with one foot, putting our weight on it as we step down, bring the other foot with a diagonal direction to a place across from the first one, and then bring the first foot over and set it down beside the second one, shifting our weight to the second foot. This ends our step, and now we simply do this over and over again.

Let's look at your dance steps separately.

Gentlemen:

First simply stand relaxed, with your feet slightly apart. Next, on the count of (1) take a step forward, heel first with your left foot, and put it down with your weight on it. Then on the count of two, step to the right with your right foot and put it down shifting, your weight onto it.

Ladies:

In the waltz, just as in the slow dance, the lady steps back on her right as the gentlemen steps toward her on his left. First, stand comfortably with your feet slightly apart. Then take a step back with your right foot on the count of (1). On the count of (2), step over to the left diagonally, putting your weight on your left foot. On the count of (3), draw your right foot close to your left foot and then put your weight on your right foot. This takes you half way through our Basic Box Step. We finish it then by stepping forward on your left foot on the count of one, over on the right on the count of two, and then drawing closed and shifting weight on the count of three. Do this over and over again. As you can see, this is very simple.

I think we are ready to try this with music. Again, we will dance in the closed position, a comfortable distance apart, determined by the young lady. This song has a long, instrumental introduction. Wait for the three-count tempo to begin. Remember, gentlemen step forward with their left foot as ladies step back on their right.

That looks very good for a start. Please be seated, and will the rest of the class please come onto the dance floor and try it? Very good, thank you.

Now to give our waltz some added dimension and more graceful feeling we will add a rotation. This is called *turning the basic step* It is a gentle, left hand or counter-clockwise rotation. When he is stepping back on his left, the gentleman turns slightly back to his left, with each step bringing the couple around in a graceful turn. Now, let's have everyone on the floor at once to try rotating the basic box step together. If this is done properly, everyone should be able to fit as all the dancers go around the room simultaneously in the same counter-clockwise rotation in the Grand Ballroom tradition.

That is all for today. Thank you.

Teens at the Table

Part II
American Cotillion

Lesson 8: Dance Floor Etiquette

Welcome to our final lesson in the American Cotillion course.

There is a lot to do, so let's get started. Ladies, quietly place yourselves in alphabetical order by last names and form a line on my left here at the front of the room. Gentlemen, also form a line alphabetically, but stand to my right. Remember the order you are in; it will be important later. Today we will practice the ballroom dances and learn more about dance floor etiquette. We will continue the Introduction to Ballroom Dance with Rumba, and Cha-Cha. If time allows, we will try Swing Dance and Rock and Roll.

Young ladies will be introduced, congratulated with a handshake for finishing the Etiquette Lessons course, and escorted to their seats.

(Instructor, please note: A parent or teacher may assist with presentations. Also, if Etiquette Certificates are awarded, they require student's name and two signatures—done in advance.) Young ladies, when I introduce you step forward, smile, then bounce a slight curtsey by bending your knees. Lift your eyes toward the back of the room and hesitate for a photo or to receive a presentation. (Other students should applaud each fellow student.) She will then look towards the right and the next young gentleman in line will step forward, extend his left elbow toward the young lady, establish eye contact with her and lead her forward to her seat.

She may link her arm in his or simply rest her right hand on his forearm so he can guide her. There he will pull the chair out for her, she will step in front of the chair, and he will push the chair in for her as she sits down, saying "Thank you." He will then return to the end of the line of young gentlemen for his introduction in turn. Once all the young ladies have been seated, the young gentlemen are introduced. They may bow slightly, look at the audience, give eye contact to the instructor with the handshake, and take their seat.

(Presentation of etiquette booklets and, or certificates may be done at this time per the Instructor's choice. Instructor may also choose to sample some treats from the final (7th) course of a banquet or select something from the tradition of High Tea and call today our *Teen Tea Dance*. See Lesson Plans) Now that you are all seated, you will notice that your places are set for dessert. That will be served a little later; for now you will receive a beverage only, because it is time to practice ballroom dances, so we will continue with the introduction to Ballroom Dance.

When the music begins we will need six couples on the dance floor to start. Will the first six young gentlemen from the escort line please stand up? Quickly ask a partner for this dance and escort her to the dance floor. The first dance will be the American slow dance. To review, this is our easy-going, beginning dance. It is ideal for getting started slowly on the dance floor. First the couple establishes a classic closed-dancing position by standing normally with feet slightly apart, facing each other. The lady's right foot is in between the man's feet. The gentleman's right hand is under the lady's left arm and below her shoulder blade, while her left arm is lying on his right arm. Her left hand is on his right shoulder, elbows lifted slightly to allow for easy movement. On the other side, their hands are in the palm-to-palm grip lifted to the lady's shoulder height so that the couple comfortably maintains upright posture. The young gentleman takes the lead always and establishes a direction for the couple by guiding with his left hand and left foot first, while rocking back and forth, either stepping side to side or forward toward the lady and then back. He simply takes two steps out and two steps back and she follows in corresponding movements, shifting their weight as they go. This is "walking to the beat of the music."

To review, the basic step of the American slow dance is easy. First, the gentleman steps toward the Lady with his left foot (1) and she steps back on her right. That shifts the weight to his left (&) and hers to her right in the first two beats of the music. He then takes a step toward her on his right foot (2), while she lifts her left foot and moves it back a step. Repeat that, and then reverse direction for 4 counts. Think as you go, 1 & 2 & 1 & 2 and 1 & 2 & 1 & 2 and. Between direction changes, keep one foot in place. Step out, rocking from side to side in a Hesitation Step to the (1) & (2) & beat. This gives the dance a more relaxed look, especially if you add a little bounce by bending the knees when you step out to the side. At some point the gentleman can begin a Rotation Step by slowly turning as he steps. Once confident in these basic steps, the couple can put them together into a simple routine of <u>Forward and Side-to-Side, then Backward and the Rotation</u>.

Halfway through the song…this is going well. Everyone looks as if they know what they are doing! Will the next six gentlemen please stand? I want you to cut in on these gentlemen and finish the dance with the young ladies who are on the floor. Will the first six gentlemen please go and ask another partner for the next dance?

All dancers will stay on the floor for the next song, which will be a waltz. To review: Just as in the slow dance, in the waltz we use the closed position, with hands held palm to palm, elbows slightly elevated to allow freedom of movement. The basic waltz step is known as the "box step" because it is like drawing a square with your feet in three-count tempo, six beats at a time: (1) (2) (3) & (1) (2) (3) & etc. Remember that you will be shifting your weight with each step and that the gentleman steps forward on his left foot as the lady steps backward with the right foot. Here we go with a waltz. Please stay on the dance floor. I'm sure you will all remember how to do the waltz. If you ever need a reminder, an excellent dance movie to watch is titled "Strictly Ballroom," It begins with the same music you have been dancing waltz to: the "Beautiful Blue Danube."

Now you will learn another slow dance featured in the musical comedy, "Strictly Ballroom": the rumba. The rumba is very much like a waltz, with a Latin beat added. The rumba was the first dance with a Latin beat introduced to American Ballrooms. It was introduced during the Big Band Era and here is one of the classic tunes that brought it to us.

This is, "The Girl From Ipanema" by Stan Getz and Astrud Gilberto. The rumba dancing position is different from the waltz in some significant ways. First, the music has an intermittent Latin drumbeat to which the dancers slightly roll the hips and shoulders, release the closed position and turn out while still holding hands, look away from each other and return to the holding position. Instead of just holding hands palm to palm, the dancers' forearms are held upright and almost touching. The man's right hand is on the lady's left shoulder blade and the lady's left arm is resting on the gentleman's right arm. Her fingertips should be approximately on his right shoulder.

The basic rumba step is two steps slowly forward, then a quick closing step to one side. We say, *Slow, slow, Quick, quick.* The count is (1) (2) (3) and (4). Again, we start with the gentleman stepping forward on his left and the lady stepping back on her right.

This is truly like walking together for two steps and then taking a step to the gentleman's right and the lady's left, slightly rolling the hips and shoulders as you shift your weight from foot to foot. The next thing you want to do is a rotation of the basic step. As before, this is done with a gentle left or counterclockwise turn as the gentleman steps back on his left foot.

Now we will add the lady's underarm turn to the Basic Step. In the closed position, this move is made halfway through the basic step after the first slow, slow and quick, quick. half-way through the basic step, the gentleman lifts his left hand up in the air. This tells the lady that she is going to do her turn. From here he continues with the rest of the basic step as the lady steps straight forward on the counts of slow, slow with her right foot and then turns out on the quick, quick to the left with her left foot first and then her weight shifting on to it, landing on the second quick. The gentleman draws her back into the closed position on the next slow, slow as she steps back on her right again. Another way to look at this is that in the lady's underarm turn, the lady simply walks under the gentleman's uplifted arm as he steps behind her. These three basic rumba steps go together to make a nice routine. Let's try it from the top. Thank you; now you may be seated. Learning rumba is a good way to become familiar with dancing to the Latin beat. There are many steps to learn and many Latin dances similar to Rumba, including the popular ChaCha and Tango.

How do you ask someone to dance?

The gentleman makes eye contact and smiles. He may extend his hand or arm to the lady, ready to lead her to the dance floor, saying her title and name and *"Would you like to dance?"* or *"May I have this dance?"*

If there are dance cards, the dances are numbered and promised ahead of time.

After the music stops, the gentleman walks with the lady back to her seat and thanks her for the dance, then helps her to be seated again. When the song is over, their agreement to be together to dance during that song ends. If the gentleman would like her to dance with him again, he must ask, "Would you like to dance again?"

A Dance Is *Only* A Dance

If she declines an offer to dance, a young lady should give a reason why she will not dance at this time.

If she declines an offer to dance with a certain young man, she should not dance with another during the same song.

The young gentleman whom she declined should stay optimistic; other young ladies might like the opportunity to dance with him.

We just have time for the Introduction to Swing Dance. Would everyone please find a partner and come to the dance floor? We will be dancing to a tune by Glenn Miller, this one is titled, **"In the Mood."**

Swing dance music has a much faster beat. It introduced a new era to Ballroom Dance with the more open dance position and lots of dips and turns. Swing dance gave the dance couple more freedom to stylize their dance, creating routines and exhibition dances. Swing brought some elements from ethnic and military music together in the ballroom to create an energetic expression of America's youth in the 1940s. It was the forerunner to the beginning of early American Rock and Roll in the 1950s.

The basic swing dance is started with the traditional closed position. When the music starts, the couple jumps into action with any one of a number of turns. For example, the gentleman lifts his left arm, then the lady pushes off from the gentleman's shoulder into an underarm turn. After turning, the lady takes his right hand in her left hand and the couple continues to dance, holding both hands. Multiple spins and turns are executed as the couple alternately pushes off and pulls together again, always holding hands. They move apart and together to the bouncing rhythm of the music, allowing for great turning flexibility with the arms. The steps are very simple: *ball/change* (1) and (2) *ball/change* (3) and (4) then (5)(6) pull back and (7)(8) move forward. The couple returns to the traditional closed position to finish the dance with a flourish. Try it; once you hear the music, you will be in the mood to dance. Remember: the gentleman extends his left hand, palm up, the lady puts her right hand in his, palm down, she smiles while giving eye-contact and puts her left hand on his shoulder. He then puts his right hand on her back below her left shoulder blade. They stand facing each other with their feet slightly apart, her right foot between his. On the count of one, she will step back on her right while he steps forward on his left.

In closing, whether we are dancing Classic Ballroom Waltzes, modern Rock & Roll with stylistic freedom, Latin, Line Dancing, Hip Hop or Salsa with gymnastics and tribal overtones on the dance floor, we must always bring to it what we have learned about traditional dance floor etiquette.

One of the greatest advantages of Ballroom dancing is that it trains one to present oneself well, to sit, stand, and walk with confidence and grace. Good Luck!

To close our session, we'll play "Rockin' Robin." This is classic Rock and Roll, with this you can feel free to use the holding position, alternately with holding hands and going freestyle, do lots of turns and Have Fun!

Sources

BOOKS

Hoving, Walter. *Tiffany's Table Manners For Teen—Agers.* New York: Ives Washburn, Inc., 1961

Johnson, Dorothea, *The Little Book of Etiquette,* Philadelphia: Running Press Publications, 1997

MAGAZINES

Talliaferro, Elizabeth, *Popovers Anytime,* Tampa: Cooking Light, 2004

West, Forest W., *The Vocabulary of Fine Dining,* Honolulu: the Pacific Club, 1992

INTERNET

http://www.canadadry.com/Recipes/EasyCranberryPunch.cfm

http://www.burrows.com/other/manners.html

VIDEOTAPE

Webb, Kyle, *Your Wedding Dance,* West Lake Village, CA: Brentwood, 1993

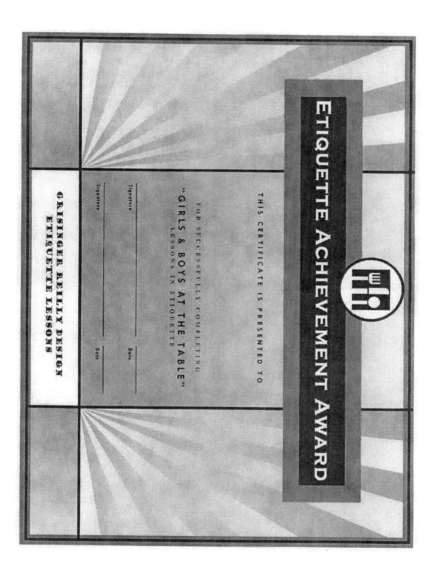

ETIQUETTE ACHIEVEMENT AWARD

THIS CERTIFICATE IS PRESENTED TO

FOR SUCCESSFULLY COMPLETING

"GIRLS & BOYS AT THE TABLE"
LESSONS IN ETIQUETTE

Signature

Signature

Date

GRISINGER REILLY DESIGN
ETIQUETTE LESSONS

Order Student Incentives for Presentation to Program Graduates

Item # 001) CERTIFICATES

Etiquette Achievement Certificates...$12.00 per doz.

Item #002) CHILDREN age 5–11yrs. ETIQUETTE BOOKLET

Titled, "Girls & Boys at the Table" by Teresa Kathryn Grisinger Reilly etiquette booklet...$1.50 ea. $18.00perdoz.

Item #003) TEENS age 12–20 yrs. ETIQUETTE BOOKLET

Titled, "Old School Charm" by Teresa Kathryn Grisinger Reilly Teens etiquette booklet...$2.25 ea. $27.00perdoz.

Item #004) MUSIC & DANCE CD...$3.95

Item #005) Quiz Book, "the Quizzer" Contains 2 new tests on each lesson plus final exams...$9.95

Send item #, quantity, description, unit price plus $3.85 per 5 items for priority mail shipping, along with check or money order to:

GRISINGER REILLY DESIGN LLC
7143 State Road 54 #215
New Port Richey, FL
34653-6104

About the Author

Teresa Kathryn Grisinger Reilly is a seventh-generation American writer, portrait artist, and graduate of the University of Oregon. She studied Art History at the Museum of Art and Tufts University in Boston and is currently working on a Masters Degree in Arts & Education. She believes that every child's ethnic heritage is woven into America's tablecloth, that traditions in fine dining bond us together and that we can strengthen and preserve our culture by teaching etiquette, good manners and ballroom dance in America's classrooms. She lives with her husband and two children in Florida on the Gulf of Mexico.

"Ours is the practical and natural approach to etiquette training. Young people study these lessons gaining confidence and skill together. They soon begin to conform to the roles of ladies and gentlemen at the table. We strive to prepare our students to dine capably and independently. We review and reinforce good manners taught at home adding nuances of fine dining etiquette. This system of dining and social behavior creates opportunities for each graduate's best traits to shine through."

Teresa Kathryn Grisinger Reilly

To contact us: call Toll-Free: (877) 847-2748

Email: ms.teresa@etiquettelessons.com

www.etiquettelessons.com

978-0-595-33198-7
0-595-33198-X

LaVergne, TN USA
06 April 2010
178253LV00003B/24/A